DEARLY BELOVED

Letters of Faith and Encouragement to Overcoming Saints

Paul & Gretel Haglin

Sovereign World

Sovereign World Ltd
PO Box 777
Tonbridge
Kent TN11 9XT
England

ISBN: 1 85240 191 5

Cover design by PAZ
Typeset by CRB Associates, Norwich, England
Printed in the USA by Dickinson Press Inc., Grand Rapids

DEDICATION

We dedicate *Dearly Beloved* to Barbara O. Jacobsen, a chum since high school, who prayed us into the Kingdom, prayed us into the Baptism of the Holy Spirit, and who tenderly prayed us out of numerous spiritual bayous along the way. Her encouragement has buoyed us up through the years, and her example of clinging to faith in Jesus through life's most challenging circumstances has constantly inspired us to "**...press on toward the goal for the prize of the upward call of God in Christ Jesus.**" (Philippians 3:14)

Thank you, Barb!

CONTENTS

FOREWORD

Paula and I have received Paul and Gretel's monthly teaching letter from their Resurrection Christian Ministries for almost 15 years now. We have greatly enjoyed reading their positive and uplifting teachings and are delighted that they have now collected many of the most potent and timely of them into this book (though it could well be twice as long!).

Sometimes we have come home from trips so exhausted from teaching and from praying for so many broken servants of the Lord that it seemed hardly possible to keep putting one foot in front of another, but Paul and Gretel's encouraging words waiting for us among our stacks of mail helped to lift the cloud of fatigue and turn our eyes back to our victorious Lord Jesus. They enabled Him to renew our energies and to restore the outlook of hope that we all need to carry with us when we teach and minister to others.

The subtitle of this book is "Letters of Faith and Encouragement to Overcoming Saints." It could just as well have been "Renewals of Faith, Hope, and Love" for that is what we and so many others have gleaned from this fruitful vineyard over the years.

Our hope and prayer is that many saints will find here nuggets that turn from the gold of simple wisdom to the bread of life that nourishes and sustains. May God bless, nourish, and refresh you as you read *Dearly Beloved.*

Yours in the love of our Lord Jesus Christ,

John and Paula Sandford

Co-Founders, Elijah House, Inc.

INTRODUCTION

Little did we dream, so many years ago (1978) when we first began to correspond on a regular basis with some of the faithful radio listeners of Paul's 15 minute, five-day a week *Letters of Faith* teaching program, that we would now be sending monthly epistles to saints in 30 different countries!

For the first five years of Paul's 13-year radio teaching ministry, no one even knew his last name because he only referred to himself as Brother Paul. He did not want to receive any kind of attention that should have been focused on the Lord and on His precious Word.

Even the members of the church we attended hadn't the faintest idea that the Paul they knew in church was the same Brother Paul that taught them over the radio at 7:45 a.m. every weekday on the way to work—until he would pray with them! Then their eyes would widen with recognition. "That voice!—are you the Brother Paul of *Letters of Faith* I listen to every day?" So the word spread, and the letters that poured into our mailbox began to be addressed to him by his last name as well.

Paul always addressed the radio listeners as "Dearly Beloved," or just "Beloved," because he imagined people's individual faces and lives as he taught. He felt that he was really speaking directly and personally to each person as though he were able to look them right in their eyes. He was not "preaching" to the masses, he was sharing with dear friends what the Lord was teaching him, and they felt his love and his care for them.

Many said that they received his scriptural teachings as though they came directly from the heart of God.

The Lord called us to pastor a fellowship that He grew out of the home prayer meeting we had hosted for many years, and soon I was helping Paul answer letters for prayer from radio listeners as well as helping pastor our fellowship. When we started mailing out a teaching letter every month we began to write them together, and as the Lord called us to teach together more and more, we also began to write some of the lessons together until the Lord blended us into a harmonious ministering partnership where the two of us have so become one that now it is hard to guess which of us wrote what *Letters of Faith* or what lesson.

We began to expand these *Letters of Faith* into full-length teachings and in 1982 God released us from pastoring our local church to travel in response to invitations from other churches who yearned to know more about how to walk with the Lord in wholeness and in godly relationship with each other. We traveled and taught all over the United States, and in 1984 we boarded our first plane to Great Britain, where we have spent six to eight weeks a year teaching and ministering in England and Wales ever since.

This book has been written in response to the many readers of our monthly *Letters of Faith*, who have asked us to compile some of their favorite letters in a form that they could keep and meditate on all year round. As we have re-read the notebooks full of *Letters of Faith* dating all the way back to 1978 to choose and re-edit the ones we felt the Lord was freshly anointing, we were astounded by how prophetic some of them are! It is our prayer that these messages will stir you deep in your spirit, lift your faith, and encourage you.

We are in awe that the Lord allowed us to keep writing these monthly meditations even through the difficult and trying times of our lives. How did we ever meet all those deadlines in the midst of so much ministry and trauma? Only by His calling and anointing —only by His grace!

We pray that you will be drawn to meditate with the Holy Spirit on these teachings from the springboard of the prayers we have included with each lesson. Allow Him to use these messages to stretch and challenge you to embrace all that Jesus has for you in the whole cup of salvation. It is our constant prayer that you may be filled with a new understanding of your partnership with Him in building the Kingdom of God in your life and in each and every person with whom you come in contact. St. Augustine is reported to have said, "Be a witness at all times and, if necessary, use words"!

We thank God for our precious secretary, Meg Sampson, and her patient husband Joel who, as members of our original Eagles Nest Fellowship, had personally saved every *Letters of Faith* we ever wrote and so preserved a record of even the very early ones!

Meg has painstakingly proofed each letter through our many re-edits, and offered her wise suggestions for the sake of clarity, brevity, and spelling. It has been a Herculean job for a young mother with a very active young daughter. Thank you, Meg. Without your help, *Dearly Beloved* would never have gone to press!

It would be remiss of us not to acknowledge the tremendously blessed influence of John and Paula Sandford in our lives. We value them not only as teachers, prophets, and authors, but as dear and faithful friends and partners in the Gospel. With them we have shared our hopes and dreams, insights and prayers as well as our home, sense of humor and strenuous forms of relaxation like tennis (even in the rain) as often as our schedules have managed to mesh. It was they who first drew us into examining God's heart and Word for healing, reconciling relationships, and transformation through prayer and Holy Spirit ministry. They prophetically confirmed our change in assignment from pastoring to traveling ministry. And they first opened pulpits in major teaching conferences for us to teach and minister together. Thank you two most beloved for sowing such love and confidence and so much of yourselves into our lives, and for remaining so genuine and real even as you have gained much deserved prominence with your ministry.

Our deepest thanks and appreciation to Lou and Lil Carey, discipleship training director at Dunklin Memorial Camp, U.S.A.F. Lt. Gen. Pat and Lauraine Caruana, and our daughter, Alexis, who have all faithfully served God and the two of us on the Board of Directors of Resurrection Christian Ministries since it was founded in 1977. Thanks too for the mutual love and support of Dick and Judy French and Jim and Shelvy Wyatt with whom we are joined in the Spirit.

We must also thank the hundreds of special saints who have encouraged us with testimonies and with financial support. *You* have kept this ministry going! Thank you—this book is really yours! We love you!

The scriptural call for all of our teachings is from Titus 1:1 as set forth in the Amplified Bible—we are called to be "**special messenger**(s) **of Jesus Christ, the Messiah, to stimulate and promote the faith of God's chosen ones and lead them on to accurate discernment and recognition of and acquaintance with the Truth which belongs to and harmonizes with and**

tends to godliness." The truth which transforms us into godliness in all of our thoughts, words, and deeds—that is where the spiritual rubber hits the road of righteousness—the highway of holiness!

We pray that this book will be a manifestation of that word in your life! We would love to hear from you.

Hugs,

Paul & Gretel Haglin

Resurrection Christian Ministries

Chapter 1

THE GOAL OF OUR INSTRUCTION

Dearly Beloved,

"My brethren, let not many of you become teachers,
knowing that we shall receive a stricter judgment.
For we all stumble in many things.
If anyone does not stumble in word, he is a perfect
man, able also to bridle the whole body."
(James 3:1–2 NKJ)

"But the goal of our instruction is love from a pure
heart and a good conscience and a sincere faith.
For some men, straying from these things,
have turned aside to fruitless discussion,
wanting to be teachers of the Law,
even though they do not understand either
what they are saying or the
matters about which they make confident assertions.
But we know that the Law is good,
if one uses it lawfully . . . "
(1 Timothy 1:5–8)

Teachers in the Body of Christ have been given special callings and giftings for communicating the truth and the Lord's heart to others. We have enjoyed observing and even meeting many of these men and women personally, some of whom have become dear friends. The ones to whom we are most attracted, however, are the ones who have studied the divine "techniques" of the greatest teacher, Jesus Christ, and by His grace have tried to emulate Him. Their lifestyles reflect the purity and humility of Jesus, and like Him you can tell immediately that they are guided by the Holy Spirit. They have learned to teach from a heart of compassion for the people.

Jesus always taught with His life as well as with His words. He was more interested in conveying His Father's character and divine plan for the coming Kingdom than arguing the finer points of doctrine, drawing an admiring crowd, or using His influence to challenge the rule of Rome.

The people who had ears to hear and eyes to see what Jesus was teaching about the reality of the Kingdom of God were inspired to follow Him to learn more of the wonderful truths He was sharing. "**...the multitudes were amazed at His teaching; for He was teaching them as one having authority, and not as their scribes.**" (Matthew 7:28–29) They recognized that He was not showing off His knowledge but demonstrating a powerful and loving sacrificial life that brings healing, deliverance, and the knowledge of God. He created a hunger for eternal life.

It has struck us how many times in His ministry Jesus felt free to use just a phrase from the Scriptures (of course, they had not been broken up into chapters and verses then!) to illustrate and give credence to a point He was making. The very mention of a phrase of familiar Scripture instantly brought back the memory of the whole passage and its context to these people who had learned so much of it by heart! Those who had ears to hear understood what He was saying and rejoiced!

It is almost heretical in some circles today to teach that way, but Jesus did it! The inspired writings were His tools which He used with familiarity, skill, and understanding. He was not afraid of applying them as the Holy Spirit directed and they came alive and pierced the hearts of those who were listening. However, His choosing and using fragments from the Scriptures never altered their meaning, or changed the basic revelation of the heart and character of His Father!

Jesus did not expound the truth of the Scriptures by ponderous systematic exegetical teaching that has become de rigueur in some church circles today. He would often scoop up a child who was playing at His feet and use him for an illustration of innocent trust, or tell a story of a farmer faithfully sowing his seeds and wondering why some do not sprout. He delighted in using trees or fields or streams as well as the actions and lives of scriptural heroes for allegorical examples. These parables held hidden spiritual meanings that transcend the literal sense.

Jesus illustrated His teachings from life around Him and warned the hardhearted "textualists" of His day, **"You search the Scriptures, because you think that in them you have eternal life; and it is these that bear witness of Me; and you are unwilling to come to Me, that you may have life."** (John 5:39–40) God, our Father, is calling us to His Son; not to a book—even the Bible—not to a religious governmental entity, not to a code of ethics, or to a prescribed ritual of worship.

At a time when the rabbis were declaring that to teach a woman the things of God from the sacred Scriptures, or Talmud, was worse than uttering an obscenity, Jesus allowed Mary to sit at His feet and learn while He shared the ways and the will of His Father. He ministered truth, forgiveness, and inner healing to a Samaritan woman of questionable moral standing, and allowed a repentant prostitute to minister to Him. Martha was counted as a friend whose home He chose as His headquarters while He ministered in

Jerusalem, because He felt comfortable there with her family. He honored and respected all men and women and children as the handiwork of His Father, and treated each with equal love and understanding.

The only seemingly harsh words Jesus ever uttered were to the religious leaders who kept their people in the bondage of darkness, ignorance, and prejudice by controlling them with rules and formulas: **"But woe to you, scribes and Pharisees, hypocrites, because you shut off the kingdom of heaven from men; for you do not enter in yourselves, nor do you allow those who are entering to go in."** (Matthew 23:13)

We who are called to be teachers in this present era must always be reminded Who is to be our ultimate example! No matter how "successful" a contemporary leader may be, or how intrigued we may be by reading about the lives of well-known saints or even Old Testament prophets, no one is to be our pattern but Jesus Christ Himself. Only the Holy Spirit, whom Jesus has sent to teach us, knows the Father's heart and the times, circumstances, and agenda of God's plan.

What might have been straight from the throne room even 25 years ago, let alone 2 or 3 millenniums ago, may not be appropriate or what is needed today to reach and return the hearts of His people to God. Even though Jesus was an historical figure we must demonstrate with our teachings that Jesus is alive today. He is not ignorant of what it means to live in this day and age and culture! Read Bruce E. Olson's *Bruchko*, an autobiographical saga of his ministry to a fierce tribe of primitive Colombian Indians, and how the Holy Spirit tenderly and sensitively guided him in reaching them for Christ. Translating concepts of Christianity must start with our demonstrating the reality of Christ in our behavior towards others in His Name.

There are times when we weep to hear on what peripheral issues some teachers are focusing. For instance, the overemphasis on the government of God and the function of the five-fold ministries has paralyzed many churches. The people have been told that they are "not in order" unless they are governed "properly" and are under the approved "head-covering!" It is interesting that Jesus seems to care far less about the state of government of the church than about our learning to govern our own spirits righteously by the power of the indwelling Holy Spirit. The Apostle Paul lists the fruit of self-control as the apex of the fruit of the Spirit in Galatians 5:22–23. (Remember that Middle-Eastern custom tends to list the best or choicest last.)

Humility, holiness, and harmony with the Father are more important than public honor. Have you noticed the proliferation of titles that have sprung up even in non-denominational circles? The elevation of a teacher/leader to a mythical bishopric office complete with the title and the donning of clerical collar and robes to lend prestige, is horrifying to us. John Wesley, the famous Anglican minister, was shocked to hear that the "authoritarian American Methodist superintendent Francis Asbury changed his title from Superintendent to Bishop. He reprimanded him, 'How can you, how dare you, suffer yourself to be called a Bishop? I shudder, I start, at the very thought! Men may call me a knave or a fool, a rascal, a scoundrel and I am content, but they shall never by my consent call me a bishop! For my sake, for God's sake, for Christ's sake put a full end to this!' " (page 124, *Root Out Of a Dry Ground: A History of the*

Church by Charles P. Schmitt, Fellowship Publications.) Charles Schmitt continues: "But unfortunately this was to be only the beginning. And Methodism's increased organizationalism inevitably caused its spiritual decline."

Leaders who have started Bible Schools on their own, conferring honorary doctoral degrees on their esteemed friends, is another trend that has built an elitism in the church, something that Jesus frowned upon and warned His disciples about! (See Mark 10:35–45) The head of one Bible School confided to us that Paul really ought to have a doctoral degree to be accepted in the "best" Christian circles and if he would just take a couple of their courses they would give him the coveted honor! Needless to say, he declined.

How the genuine academic society mocks those that put on such airs! Those we know who have earned a genuine doctorate in their field, (except physicians of course), seldom allow anyone to use that designation on any but the most formal occasions because it is considered ostentatious or "tacky."

The lack of Jesus' qualifying credentials did not seem to hold Him back! Someone like Billy Graham, however, who is so obviously anointed and has walked in the Lord without a trace of scandal or error, has rightly been awarded honorary degrees from prestigious universities as well-deserved recognition from the whole Body of Christ for his faithfulness and impact on the whole world. He rarely uses titles, however, preferring just to be called Billy!

Jesus referred to Himself as the Son of Man and wore an unadorned robe. He pointed out in Matthew 23:6–7 that the scribes and Pharisees "**...love the place of**

honor at banquets, and the chief seats in the synagogues, and respectful greetings in the market places, and being called by men, Rabbi." (Read Rabbi as Father, Bishop, Apostle, or Doctor today!) He warned them in verse 12: "**. . . whoever exalts himself shall be humbled; and whoever humbles himself shall be exalted."** And for the rest of the chapter we read verse after verse that starts with: **"Woe to you, scribes and Pharisees . . ."**

The sin of elevating men and women to prominent positions of honor above the rest of the believers ought to make us tremble and fall at His feet in deep repentance and fear of the Lord on behalf of the whole Body of Christ. That kind of pre-eminence almost always leads to a ruling class that grows deaf and blind to the needs of the people and to the heart of God, and will eventually suppress the "laity" in order to keep their position of "clerical" control. No wonder Jesus hated the deeds and teachings of the Nicolaitans! ("niko" meaning: conquer or suppress; and "laites" meaning: the people. See Revelation 2:6 & 15)

The heavier the anointing on teachers, the more they ought to seek the way of the simple life of Jesus! Time spent alone studying and hearing from the Spirit of God should not be a last-minute squeeze before a meeting or teaching session. Rather than holding themselves aloof before or after a service, teaching ministers ought to walk in and among the people to hear what God has placed on the peoples' hearts. It is important to understand where they are spiritually. Jesus walked with His Father in the midst of the people whom They deeply loved and cared for.

He will do the same for any of us who humbly ask Him and determine in our hearts to seek His face,

His kingdom, and His righteousness before anything else.

Hugs,

Paul and Gretel

Lord Jesus, show me how my life can be a
living teaching of Your love, of Your heart purity,
and of a sincere faith that is pleasing to You.
Please Jesus, guard me from pride or any of the
worldly practices that would in any way detract from
the power of Your Gospel.
Thank You for the lives of precious brothers and
sisters that You graced to be bright and shining stars
in the darkness of their own generations.
Let me be such a one as they
to all those You have
reading my life.
Amen.

Chapter 2

HE HEALS THE BROKENHEARTED

Dearly Beloved,

"The righteous cry and the Lord hears,
And delivers them out of all their troubles.
The Lord is near to the brokenhearted,
And saves those who are crushed in spirit."
(Psalm 34:17–18)

There was a time for us personally when our whole world seemed to be coming apart at the seams for a period of two nightmarish years of draconian circumstances. Our business was taken away from us by unscrupulous men and with it (we thought) our God-designed opportunity to support not only our family but many individual ministers in the Body of Christ. Our reputation was lost.

The wonderful, exciting Church to which we belonged "blew up" and we were accused falsely of "siding with the enemy" and asked not to prophesy or pray for anyone anymore—we who were reconcilers! Our reputation was lost.

Our elder son was so disillusioned with not only the business world and its unfair practices but the Body of Christ for its insensitivity, that he chucked it all and walked out into the subculture of the drug world just three weeks before his high school graduation. Our reputation was lost.

During this time, we had let the Lord fashion a vital church out of our home prayer group. Within months Paul almost died from internal bleeding and only an emergency operation, 13 pints of blood, and much prayer saved his life. The day he was released from the hospital our worship leader, fortified by a popular local evangelist, came to accuse Paul of not having enough faith to be healed and therefore not having the required qualifications to be his pastor any longer. He eventually convinced two-thirds of our church to join him at the young evangelist's newly formed "spiritually correct" faith church. Our reputation was lost!

It seemed as though we were bombarded with one blow after another and it took all the faith and energy we had to just take each day as it came, caring for our family and the decimated flock, and trying to reconstruct our lives into some semblance of stability and usefulness. Our reputation was lost, and our hearts were broken!

Then one Sunday a precious saint came running up to me with the exciting news that she had just seen a vision during worship. She said that she saw the giant hand of God, and in the center of His palm were huddled two cracked, grey, and lifeless-looking hearts. The only thing preventing them from falling apart into pieces was the fact that they were leaning against one another. She saw a large tear drop from above and bathe them both, as though God was suffering with them! He said to her that those two hearts, propping each other up inside His loving palm, were Paul and Gretel.

Our friend then heard a soft, soothing humming such as a mother would use to comfort a hurting child, and she saw God's large forefinger gently running up and down the jagged edges of the fissures in our hearts. As it did, the damaged flesh miraculously knit together! The dull grey hue was replaced by a healthy pink, and the hearts began to pulse vigorously again, until they fairly glowed in the Lord's hand.

Suddenly, as Jo Ann was speaking forth this prophetic vision, the pain that had gripped the inside of my chest left as if it were wrenched out of me, and I felt a surge of joy and hope fill me. The pain was gone! I felt life course through my whole body! I ran to Paul and exitedly described her vision and what had happened to me, and as he listened, he saw the same vision, and his broken heart was healed instantly as well!

As we stood hugging each other in relief and freedom, laughing and crying and praising the Lord, God quietly made known to us that He wanted us to remember this experience of His healing our broken hearts forever. *"We will never forget!"* we cried out to Him together!

It was then that we were aware that He was giving us a choice: whether to walk in our healing, carefully guarding our newly-mended hearts and resisting having to ever relive that kind of pain, or, putting our trust in Him, reopening our hearts to love, aware that they might be broken again in His service, but assured of His faithfulness and that if He healed so great a pain once He would do it again.

We were so overwhelmed with the graciousness and the reality of His love's healing that we eagerly agreed together to allow Him to use us to love others again—come what may!

At that moment both of us felt God's presence embracing us and we understood Him to say, *"Through and for Me, risk loving the unlovely, and those who snarl at My name, and those who are in opposition to you, even those who despitefully use you, that they might come to know My love is unconditional. You will suffer more broken hearts, but I promise to heal you when you cry out to Me, and each time I heal your heart* ***I will make your heart stronger, not harder!***"

Adversity builds character when we Christians choose to face and deal with it in Jesus Christ, until loving and forgiving and forgetting becomes second nature to us. 1 Corinthians 13:5 becomes so real that we are not even tempted to let bitterness and resentment rule our lives anymore, because love "**does not act unbecomingly; it does not seek its own** (way), **is not provoked, does not take into account a wrong suffered...**"

But as yet imperfect humans, we tend to flinch at having to suffer the pain of humiliation, rejection, judgment, ridicule, and character assassination that is so often the result of our challenging New Age "truth" that unbelievers insist is "correct", with what we know is THE TRUTH. To be honest, many of us suffer simply because of people's thoughtlessness and lack of sensitivity, and we are sorely tempted to embrace a "Poor Me" spirit. In self pity, we often think of ourselves as victims of the world rather than "more than conquerors" for the Kingdom, and we seek an excuse to avoid contact with those who make us uncomfortable.

Again, let me share a vision that the Lord showed me of my own heart to illustrate this tendency we all have to flee any meaningful "interpersonal relationships."

In this vision my heart was shown to me to be like the Temple with three distinct areas: two rooms and a courtyard. Jesus, Himself, was seated on a throne in the Holy of Holies, the innermost room of my heart, and in front of Him was a footstool that I knew was there just for me to come and sit on and worship Him and fellowship with Him in intimate privacy. The Holy

Place, the outer room of my heart, looked like a cozy living room through which the Holy of Holies could be reached. The greater area outside was like a courtyard in which I saw people milling around doing various everyday things.

The startling discovery for me, however, was that the walls of my cozy living room were covered with dozens of doors—all nailed shut with planks of wood!

"*Why?*" I asked.

And the Lord said, "*Gretel, at different times of your life you invited people into your heart to share your friendship. One way or another, they offended you, or disappointed you, or hurt you with their words or actions.*"

Immediately I had a picture of people replacing the pictures on the wall, spilling Coca-Cola on the tables, rearranging the furniture, grinding dropped food into the carpets, and leaving my precious books open in a jumble with their paper jackets carelessly ripped—disrupting my quiet nest. I was shocked and infuriated by their behavior! I saw myself firmly hustling them out the doors—and out of my life—one by one, and then determinedly nailing those doors shut with large nails that I pounded into wooden boards crossed over the door. When I finished sealing them shut, I symbolically brushed off my hands and declared aloud, "*There! That's that!*"

In the next scene, I was in "the courtyard" going about doing the usual everyday shopping and mingling when I came across a person that I had banished from my heart. I acknowledged their existence with a nod and a pleasantry, and passed by. No longer did they deserve to be privy to my secrets or to be given more than a perfunctory greeting. I had successfully cut them off from a meaningful relationship. Never again would they be so close to me that their actions or words could hurt me or affect me adversely.

Then, I saw myself back in my "living room." I realized that there was hardly anyone there but members of my close family—and even a couple of those were missing, having been ostracized from my heart for some kind of unacceptable behavior! The room was neat and tidy—and lonely!

As I stood in the middle room of my heart, I heard the voice of my Beloved from the Holy of Holies, my secret place where He and I spent such sweet time together.

"Gretel," He called out, *"Gretel, do you really love Me?"*

"Oh yes, Jesus, You know that I do!"

"Am I truly Lord of your life?"

"Jesus, I would do anything You asked of me, You know that!"

"Am I, then, the Host of your heart?"

"Of course, Lord, You are the Lord of Hosts, the Host of all I have and all I am!"

"Then open up the doors of your heart again, Gretel. Yank out those nails and tear off those wooden bars so you can throw open the doors of your heart."

"LORD! Do you have any idea what would happen if I did that?! Why, those people would come crowding in again and try to take over my life, and mess up my precious living room. I don't want anything more to do with them!" (Hey, let's get real! If you think it, you might as well tell God because He already knows it! And when you do say it, you hear how really dumb it sounds, and how un-Christlike and unloving our thoughts can become.)

There proceeded to be a silence that made me feel

increasingly uncomfortable. *"Lord?"* I called out a bit tremulously, *"Are You still there? Do You understand why I feel I cannot do what You asked me to do?"*

"Gretel, am I Lord of your life?" was all that I heard.

"Of course!" I assured Him—again! A bit more concerned this time.

2 Timothy 2:24–25 suddenly flashed into my memory: **" . . . the Lord's bond-servant must not be quarrelsome, but be kind to all, able to teach, patient when wronged, with gentleness correcting those who are in opposition . . . "**

And I heard the Lord say, *"Every door that you slammed shut was bolted with resentment, every nail that you pounded was forged in revenge, every wooden bar that you nailed up was fashioned in bitterness. As you separated yourself from these people, you separated yourself from Me. You see, Gretel, as Host and Lord of your life, I have invited certain people into your heart whom I think you need to have in your life at a particular time. Some were chosen for your companionship, others were to be your models, still others were to show you your impatience, or your prejudice, or your unwillingness to change. I sent some to spur you on, while some were sent to test your love. All were 'litmus tests' of the sincerity of your faith."*

"Oh, no!" I wailed, convicted of my unloving behavior, *"I've acted just like a heathen! Forgive me Lord for my self-centered judgment, and grant me repentance! Help me to open each door into my life and trust that it is You who will bring the people You know I need to relate to in order to be changed into Your Image. Grant me discernment not to be seduced into a victim mentality again, and give me the courage to prevent anyone from*

coming into my heart that You have not invited, please."

I am so very grateful that the Lord lovingly showed me how I had let fear lead me into self-righteousness. He has granted me forgiveness and healed me and is teaching me to discern!

We are both very grateful that the Lord lovingly showed us His faithfulness to heal our hearts—our hurts! Sure there is pain, but there is great gain in grace. The pain is for but a moment, a night, and there is great joy in the morning of each new day.

Our testimony is the Psalmist's boast from Psalm 147:3 & 5 & 7A (Amp.): **"He heals the brokenhearted and binds up their wounds—curing their pains and their sorrows. Great is our Lord, and of great power; His understanding is inexhaustible and boundless. Sing to the Lord with thanksgiving . . . !"**

Beloved, the Lord will heal YOUR broken heart and free YOU to be His witness to a brokenhearted world. He will do it because He loves you, not just to make another evangelist for His Kingdom!

He will heal your brokenness to present you to His Father whole and perfect and mature in Him as a trophy of His grace and love and sacrifice. And, Beloved, He will use you to heal the broken hearts of others!

Let Him do it!

Hugs,

Paul & Gretel

Dear Lord Jesus, please reveal to me all of the areas of my heart that I have boarded up and closed off to the people that You wanted me to welcome. Forgive me for taking offense and for not yielding my hurts to Your healing. Heal my heart, and make it stronger, but not harder, I pray! Amen.

Chapter 3

THE UPWARD CALL

Dearly Beloved,

"...press on toward the goal for the prize of the upward call of God in Christ Jesus."
(Philippians 3:14)

We have been led to meditating on sequential passages like this one from the Epistles that reveal the progression that our Father God has called us to in our understanding of who we are in Christ—**"the upward call"**!

There are higher levels of faith that we are encouraged to stretch our spiritual muscles to reach. And each time we obtain a new knowledge and faith in our oneness with Jesus Christ and have walked in it in awe and joy, the heavens part and we are privileged to catch a glimpse of yet another exciting level awaiting us ahead.

Let your eyes visually follow the flight of faith steps that the Apostles have opened for us who yearn not only to become more like Him, but to participate in the work of the Kingdom with Him:

↗ 7. **"Partakers of the divine nature"** (2 Peter 1:4)
↗ 6. **"Partakers of His discipline"** (Hebrews 12:8}
↗ 5. **"Partakers of the Holy Spirit"** (Hebrews 6:4)
↗ 4. **"Partakers of Christ"** (Hebrews 3:14)
↗ 3. **"Partakers of a heavenly calling"** (Hebrews 3:1)
↗ 2. **"Partakers of grace"** (Philippians 1:7)
↗ 1. **"Partakers of the promise"** (Ephesians 3:6)

The Father has created us to be partakers of His glory and His love with His only Son, Jesus. Our prayer for the Church today is that the revelation of this truth might grab hold of your "exciter" deep within you (that's the part that motivates you to believe and persevere!) so you will fulfill the Apostle Paul's prayer: **"If then you have been raised up with Christ, keep seeking the things above, where Christ is . . ."** (Colossians 3:1)

It is an exhilarating adventure to walk in the Spirit, learning the "trade" at the side of our Master. He will teach us what it means to be a fellow worker with Him, a partaker of His life, and a fellow heir with Him of the promises of God.

We pray that we might be able to convey to you how very much our Lord Jesus Christ wants to share His life and work with you. He longs to fellowship with you, not only just in your prayer closet, but out in the marketplace doing His work together: you in Him and He in you, enjoying one another's company and sharing secrets, and seeing the Kingdom of God being displayed in awesome ways. But **"Can two walk together, except they be agreed?"** (Amos 3:3 KJV)

God's proving ground is where the action is; where God is pouring out His Holy Spirit to set the captives free; where the character of Jesus is formed in us; where we see the sort of stuff we are made of, as we join Him in exerting all we have learned at His knee in our quiet time with Him, into the business of establishing His Kingdom here on earth, person by person.

Suddenly, all that we Christians have learned about Jesus in our early morning quiet time with Him makes sense as we see **"the prince of the power of the air, of the spirit that is now working in the sons of disobedience"** (Ephesians 2:2) being run out of people's lives because we are **"working together with Him . . . giving no cause for offense in anything . . ."** (2 Corinthians 6:1a & 3a) Awesome!

At the first level, He shows us the joy of being **"partakers of the promise"** given to His chosen ones. We still are in awe of the magnitude of His riches toward us who believe! But there is more to know about Him than this entry-level understanding of Him as a God that keeps His promises and bestows blessings on us whom He has saved from death.

At the second level, He demonstrates the power of His grace by transforming our hearts. His love floods in and begins to erode our selfishness. How we love to be **"partakers of His grace"** as we are searching for the course that He has designed for us, for we DO make mistakes! He rescues us and forgives us time after time, and, because of His gentle grace and the holy hope He has for us, we are encouraged to press on to the next level of faith and trust in Him.

At the third level, He begins to stir in us a longing to press on toward the upward call of God in Christ Jesus. We've come to realize with surprise that some things are expected of US by the One who has bought us with a terrible price—WE are to be **"partakers of a heavenly calling,"** responding to the invitation to participate in His work with Him. As this truth sinks in, we yearn to **"press on in order that** (we) **may lay hold of that for which also** (we were) **laid hold of by Christ Jesus."** (Philippians 3:12) in order that we might be a useful servant and a faithful friend.

At the fourth level, we realize that we cannot obtain the goal our heart desires without forgetting what lies behind and immersing ourselves in the now with Him who is very present. An eternally important decision has to be made, for we now must choose to become **"partakers of Christ"** in all areas of our lives.

Then, at the fifth level, He fills us with and immerses us in His Holy Spirit; making us **"partakers of the Holy Spirit"** and sends US out to **"heal the sick, raise the dead, cleanse the lepers, cast out demons; freely you received, freely give."** (Matthew 10:8) We go, in fear and trembling, very much aware that it is the Holy Spirit residing in us that is doing the works but, nevertheless, that it is WE who must be willing to be sent out in His name and it is WE who might be criticized, ridiculed, and humiliated. Our faith in His faithfulness spurs us on.

Because we have been allowed to be fellow workers with Him, the sixth step is a tall one—we must be willing to suffer by becoming **"partakers of His discipline"** as well, for **"He disciplines us for our good, that we may share His holiness."** (Hebrews 12:10) Fortunately, by this time in our walk, we understand that discipline does not mean punishment, but correction and training that develops self-control, character, orderliness, and efficiency. This may entail His saying "No" or "Not yet," when we have prayed that He will say "Yes." We learn that He loves us enough to risk our love to accomplish what needs to be accomplished in us. The truth is that *"to hurry God is to find fault with Him!"*

At the final level, we are ready to become **"partakers of the divine nature,"** for the character of Jesus Christ has been transforming our souls just as He transformed our spirits back at the threshold of our journey. Partaking means to become involved intimately with someone by sharing in their actions as well as their thoughts. What could be more satisfying than to exhibit the character of Jesus Christ to the world through our lives? Let us remember that it is good to remind each other, as well as ourselves, that God offers a deeper and deeper relationship with Him which should lead to an active and useful life modeling His Son, Jesus.

God's hope for us is that we would reach the highest level of life here on this earth. To that end, He moves heaven and earth on our behalf to thwart the enemy that would rain down upon us thoughts of despair, hopelessness, frustration, fear, confusion, and failure. All of heaven is cheering us on, urging us to stretch up to the higher mark every day until we obtain all that He has for us.

Go for it!!

Hugs,

Paul & Gretel

Lord Jesus, I am in awe of the heavenly calling
that You are urging me to accept.
The goal is so tantalizing and so grand
that I find my "spiritual adrenaline"
beginning to stir my will!
Oh precious Lord, stretch out Your hand
that I might grasp it for courage,
strength, and stamina.
Although I yearn to bound up the steps
two at a time to embrace You,
grant me patience and energy to fulfill
every phase of each level
step by step, day by day, and hour by hour,
knowing that the effort and discipline will bring
an eternal reward with You.
Amen.

Chapter 4

LOVE IS NOT JEALOUS

Dearly Beloved,

"You shall not covet
your neighbor's house; you shall not covet
your neighbor's wife or
his male servant or his female servant or
his ox or his donkey or
anything that belongs to your neighbor."
(Exodus 20:17)

"...Jealousy is as severe as Sheol;
its flashes are flashes of fire..."
(The Song of Solomon 8:6)

"...(Pilate) **was aware that the chief priests had delivered Him up because of envy."**
(Mark 15:10)

King Solomon knew only too well the power of covetousness, jealousy and envy to destroy harmony and trust, not only within a family and among friends, but between nations. He had witnessed his half-brothers increasingly being consumed with ungodly covetousness and unrestrained jealousy and envy over their father David's God-appointed position as King of Israel. They not only tried to steal the throne from their father while he was still alive, but they also succeeded in murdering some of their brothers, whom they considered to be rivals. Then, because Solomon had acquired innumerable waspish wives and quarreling concubines, he had to contend with a gaggle of jealous women and their squabbling offspring, all of whom were constantly vying for his attention and favor. (See Proverbs 21:9 & 19, 25:24, 27:4 & 15 to obtain his observations and wisdom on the subject!)

The English word "jealous" springs forth from an archaic word that meant "zeal." Our dictionary defines "jealous" as having three distinct meanings:

1. *"Very watchful or careful in guarding or keeping."* Our God is jealous ***for*** His name and He wants us to honor His name: "**. . . I shall be jealous for My holy name.**" (Ezekiel 39:25) He wants us to protect the reputations of our fellow believers in the same way. The Apostle Paul writes in 2 Corinthians 11:2: "**For I am jealous for you with a godly jealousy; for I betrothed you to one husband, that to Christ I might present you as a pure virgin.**"

2a. *"Resentfully suspicious of a rival or a rival's influence."* "**. . . the people from the cities in the vicinity of Jerusalem were coming together, bringing people who were sick or afflicted with unclean spirits; and they were all being healed. But the high priest rose up, along with all his associates, and they were filled with jealousy; and they laid hands on the apostles, and put them in a public jail.**" (Acts 5:16–18)

2b. *"Resentfully envious."* "**Now when Rachel saw that she bore Jacob no children, she became jealous of her sister . . .**" (Genesis 30:1a)

2c. *"Resulting from such feelings, for instance: a jealous rage."* "**For jealousy enrages a man, and he will not spare in the day of vengeance.**" (Proverbs 6:34) After Jesus deliberately healed the man's withered hand in front of the Pharisees in the synagogue on the Sabbath, Luke 6:11 records that the Pharisees became murderous instead of rejoicing with the restored man.

"But they themselves were filled with rage, and discussed together what they might do to Jesus."

3. "(Now rare) *Requiring exclusive loyalty ('The Lord is a jealous God. . . ')."* Even the writers of our dictionary recognized the uniqueness of this kind of righteous jealousy. Here are a few reference verses for your study: Exodus 20:5, 34:14; Deuteronomy 4:24, 5:9, 6:15; Joshua 24:19.

There is a jealous fear that tries to grip some Christians' hearts when we see supernatural favor on the heads of other men or women with results that are so remarkable that crowds of people are drawn to seek them for God's blessing. Soon, consumed with covetousness and spurred on by envy, we can be tempted to plot ways to have the prominent ones cast down and have ourselves lifted up in their stead by means of manipulation and deceit. **"And the next Sabbath nearly the whole city assembled to hear the word of God. But when the Jews saw the crowds, they were filled with jealousy, and began contradicting the things spoken by Paul, and were blaspheming."** (Acts 13:44–45) **"And some of them were persuaded and joined Paul and Silas, along with a great multitude...But the Jews, becoming jealous and taking along some wicked men from the market place, formed a mob and set the city in an uproar . . ."** (Acts 17:4 & 5)

If we allow our minds to dwell on the "unfairness" of someone else being mightily anointed, talented or gifted, good-looking, wealthy, or popular, we can soon fail to see anything right about them, and begin to attack them with a ferocity that is without logic or limit.

The picture is that of going "crabbing" on the East coast. It is no problem to keep the little critters from crawling out of your lidless basket after you've added the second crab. If one of the crustaceans begins to get near the top, it is sure to be dragged back down by the others in their mad scramble to get to the top first. The result? None of them succeed in breaking away from their open-air prison!

We Christians must resist the temptation to drag the name of someone down in an effort to prevent them from drawing all of the attention away from us, or of thinking that if we spread "a little gossip" about them, we might look good by comparison. WRONG!

Proverbs 27:4 describes the terror of unleashed jealousy: **"Wrath is fierce and anger is a flood, but who can stand before jealousy?"** It is no wonder that the spirit of jealousy is called "the green-eyed monster!" The unchecked emotion and the bitter bile of paranoia can suddenly become more than anyone can control, and it drowns those who stand in its way. It desires to "conquer or kill" for its own preservation or promotion.

This kind of conduct must be confronted immediately wherever and whenever it displays its ugly tongue or hand. The longer its twisted thoughts are allowed to run wild in our imagination, the more exaggerated the charges in our minds become against our so-called "rival," the angrier we are liable to become, and the more our dreams of revenge seem to be justified.

From the 1930s, the German nation was slowly beguiled (actually they were taken over by a demonic principality) to believe that the Jews were somehow too powerful politically and too "lucky" financially, and therefore had become detrimental to the rest of the population. Outlandish rumors were spread about them and believed even by Christians! Although individually they had been friends and neighbors and fellow workers with the Jews, and knew them to be honest and godly, the Germans corporately turned on them with a jealous rage fired by envy and hate.

Christians are not immune to the gripping, ripping talons of jealousy. Jesus' brother, the Apostle James, observed Christians wrestling with jealousy even after they were converted, and he tried to show them the devastation that occurs when they give in to that spirit, and how to prevent it from establishing a foothold in the fledgling church (James 3:13–16): **"Who among you is wise and understanding? Let him show by his good behavior his deeds in the gentleness of wisdom. But if you have bitter jealousy and selfish ambition in your heart, do not be arrogant and so lie against the truth. This** (so called) **wisdom is not that which comes down from above, but is earthly, natural, demonic. For where jealousy and selfish ambition exist, there is disorder and every evil thing."**

Thinking we are receiving Godly "wisdom," we can be driven to "warn" others of the hypocrisy, heretical teaching or proud attitude of our perceived rivals, even though we may never have met them!

Do you see covetousness, jealousy, and envy at work in your family, your church, your friendships, or your job? If you dream of ways to "show someone a lesson" or imagine them messing up and therefore losing their following; if you taste the bile of criticism rising in your throat when you see someone minister well or even look good; or if you are inundated by waves of anger when you hear a name because of a perceived injustice done to you, it is time that you cried out to God for mercy and for the gift of repentance for your sins of covetousness, jealousy, and envy!

It is imperative that you confess to a prayer partner, or to your pastor or counselor, or to some other godly person who can be used to set you free (James 5:16): **"Therefore, confess your sins to one another, and pray for one another, so that you may be healed."** The beguiling power of covetousness, jealousy, and envy is so strong that you can not set yourself free!

The Apostle Paul shared his concern for the spread of this kind of contention in 2 Corinthians 12:20: **"For I am afraid that perhaps when I come I may find you to be not what I wish and may be found by you to be not what you wish; that perhaps there may be strife, jealousy, angry tempers, disputes, slanders, gossip, arrogance,** (and) **disturbances . . ."** This concern haunted him and brought him to his knees in supplication to the Lord and he exhorted the saints in Romans 13:13, **"Let us behave properly . . . not in carousing and drunkenness, not in sexual promiscuity and sensuality, not in strife and jealousy."**

Most jealousy springs from a spirit of competitiveness that tells us that we have to fight for the crumbs God has to offer. Most of us have not grasped the vastness of God's abundant and exciting love, generosity, and boundless provision towards us (1 Corinthians 12:4–7): **"Now there are varieties of gifts, but the same Spirit. And there are varieties of ministries, and the same Lord. And there are varieties of effects, but the same God who works all things in all persons. But to each one is given the manifestation of the Spirit for the common good."**

No one is left off the gift list (as long as they are on the guest list!), or doomed to suffer the humiliation of being the last one picked to be on the team. The Apostle Paul knew that unless we can grasp the horror of the power of jealousy to destroy relationships (even between God and us, because we often blame Him for favoring others over us) and defy its siren call to attack, we have the devilish potential of being used to spread strife, resentment, and hate among innocent people, and so bring shame upon ourselves and the name of our precious Lord Jesus. That's scary!

Jesus called us to a higher realm of responsible relationship than even the writers of the Old Testament taught. He said, **"This is My commandment, that you love one another, just as I have loved you."** (John 15:12) That kind of Christian love harbors only thoughts of good for our fellow human beings because as Paul writes in 1 Corinthians 13:4 **"Love . . . is not jealous . . ."**

2 Corinthians 13:11 is a prayer we would like to pray for each of you: **"Finally,** [Beloved], **rejoice, be made complete, be comforted, be like-minded, live in peace; and the God of love and peace shall be with you."**

Gone will be the misconception that you have to fight for your blessing.

Don't let anything, or anyone, rob you of your peace from God! Walk in righteousness, peace, and joy in the Holy Spirit! ***That*** is the Kingdom walk!

Hugs,

Paul & Gretel

Loving Father, God of Love, I am ashamed of the times
I have allowed jealousy to direct my
thoughts and actions.
I am grieved by the remembrances of
envious and covetous thoughts.
Please forgive me!
Strengthen my conscience to reject the
lure of the "green-eyed monster."
Amen.

Chapter 5

NO CAUSE FOR OFFENSE

Dearly Beloved,

"And working together with Him,
we also urge you not to receive
the grace of God in vain...
giving no cause for offense in anything,
in order that the ministry be not discredited,
but in everything commending ourselves
as servants of God,

- **in much endurance**, ability to stand pain, distress, fatigue; fortitude
- **in afflictions**, implies pain, suffering, or distress imposed by illness, loss, or misfortune
- **in hardships**, things hard to bear; causes of discomfort or suffering, as poverty, pain
- **in distresses**, implies mental or physical strain imposed by pain, trouble, and worry
- **in beatings**, punishments by striking repeatedly and hard; whip, flog, or spank
- **in imprisonments**, to jail; to restrict, limit, or confine in any way
- **in tumults**, great emotional disturbances; agitation of mind or feeling
- **in labors**, physical or mental exertions; work, toil
- **in sleeplessness**, unable to sleep; wakeful, restless
- **in hunger..."** wanting or needing food.

(2 Corinthians 6:1 & 3–5)

The Apostle Paul is very clear that he does not consider any of these calamities as unusual for a

Christian to encounter in the course of his or her life, nor does he consider them an acceptable excuse for giving an offense that would discredit or disgrace the ministry of the Gospel.

But some would surely say, "If we are 'good' Christians who have been 'rightly' taught how to rebuke the devil and pray down heaven, these kinds of dreadful catastrophes will not touch us or our families! Right?" "WRONG!"

The Apostle Paul, a "mighty man of faith and power," was honestly letting it be known that even righteous Christians suffer setbacks in their lives. He understood that because we live in a sin-filled world, we Christians are going to be susceptible to any one of these traumas just like the unbelievers, and we must prepare ourselves beforehand not to "cut and run" from the truth of the gospel. **"Working together with Him,"** as **"servants of God,"** our visible, righteous behavior proves to the world that this **"grace of God"** has not been given in vain to those whom He chose to be His.

The Apostle Paul obviously was shocked to find that some of the Corinthians did not conduct themselves in a godly manner when confronted with trials and were giving offense with their actions and words. They were thereby discrediting the good news that God changes people's hearts and that these heart changes can be seen in the daily lives of believers. If Jesus lives within us, what spills out from us when we are jarred by any unexpected event or action should be holy actions, not unredeemed, unholy reactions.

The Apostle Paul goes on to say (in verses 6–10) that there are temptations to let down our resolve to be righteous in all things when our lives seem to be going quite well too: **"in purity, in knowledge, in patience, in**

kindness, in the Holy Spirit, in genuine love, in the word of truth, in the power of God; by the weapons of righteousness for the right hand and the left...". He warns us not to be tripped up "**by glory and dishonor, by evil report and good report;**" or even when we are "**regarded as deceivers and yet true; as unknown yet well-known, as dying yet behold, we live; as punished yet not put to death, as sorrowful yet always rejoicing, as poor yet making many rich, as having nothing yet possessing all things.**"

We are in awe of the quiet spirit of trust in God's faithfulness that permeates the testimonies of the Christians we know personally who are living through crushing adversities even today. Their hope and love in the Lord has brought them peaceful hearts and prevented bitterness from taking root in their lives. Rather than causing offense by blaming God or other men for their misfortune, they have grown in their knowledge of God as they have sought His comfort and strength to live through Him during the dark times.

Many believers, as well as unbelievers, have lost what were once considered secure jobs, or have lost their savings or their homes because of worldwide financial circumstances or other people's greed or carelessness. To their credit, many saints have not shaken their fists at God, but have testified of their trust in Him to be with them as they vigorously seek new and meaningful employment. God's kindly provision during the lean and waiting times is astounding. Many of these suffering saints have reached out as God's servants to help those less fortunate than themselves and found God showering their efforts with peace of mind and answered prayers. Not all have found jobs yet, but we are convinced that God is arranging a place for them,

"For we are His workmanship, created in Christ Jesus for good works, which God prepared before hand, that we should walk in them." (Ephesians 2:10)

Many of you are aching over the unloving words and actions of members of your own families or churches that have caused painful hurts and memories. Only God can unravel the ugly knots and heal your battered hearts. Don't give in to the temptation to name-call or seek revenge. "Jesus knows how you feel, call out to Him and resolve to partner with Him in prayer on their behalf and watch Him work!" has been the testimony of so many who have written to us.

There are those who are struggling with mental, emotional, or physical problems. The Apostle Paul does not say, "If only there weren't sin in your life...," or "You obviously need deliverance...," or "If only you had enough faith..., God would heal you." Rather, He is simply stating that ***when*** you are suffering these afflictions, yoke yourself with God and let His grace carry you through. The Holy Spirit will let you know if an unrepentant sin or a stubborn demon is standing in the way, and how to deal with it, but in the meantime, reach up and take the hand of Jesus and walk through it with Him.

Joni Eareckson Tada has chosen to be God's servant, not an embittered woman angry at God for her paralyzed body. Her sweet spirit has led many all over the world to ask Jesus to be their Lord.

Dennis Bennett, Leonard LeSourd, and Phillip Keller all lost their beloved spiritual partners and wives to early deaths in the midst of their ministry during the Charismatic revival, but they did not abandon the truth of what they were teaching. Instead, they turned to the Lord for strength and comfort thanking God that they would see their precious ones again one day in heaven. They went on proving the reality of the Gospel in their lives as they were planting for the Kingdom here on earth.

Corrie ten Boom, by the grace of God, refused to let hate dictate her actions and spent her time in a concentration camp encouraging others in the Lord. She was able to forgive the cruel Nazi guards who humiliated and killed her sister Betsie, and God sent her, a 60-year-old single woman, all over the earth with the message of Christian love and forgiveness.

Tim Hansel, a dedicated Christian youth leader in California, who taught inner-city kids trust by taking them mountain climbing, suffered a cataclysmic fall into a deep chasm. The permanent damage to his spine causes him to live in constant, almost unbearable pain, yet he is still encouraging people of all ages to join him on the mountains where he has a chance to witness to the reality of knowing Jesus. His book, *You Gotta Keep Dancin'*, is an inspirational teaching on living in honest faith in the midst of tribulation.

Elisabeth Elliot chose to forgive the cannibals in Ecuador who killed her missionary husband. She risked her own life to return to them and bring them the Good News with astounding results: her husband's murderer is now a fervent evangelist for Jesus Christ.

Billy Graham has preached the Gospel for decades and is a recipient of many accolades, yet there has not been even a whisper of scandal concerning him, because he has been determined to partner with God at all times! What a triumph for Christianity!

May we all urge each other to remember that we have received the grace of God to help us present the character and life of Jesus no matter what situations or temptations we face. If we really love one another, we will even risk friendships to correct each other's thinking when it starts to deviate from the truth of God's word. At the same time, we will remind each other that it is "**'not by might nor by power, but by My Spirit,' says the Lord of hosts**" (Zechariah 4:6b) that we are able to remain lights in the darkness and salt to a jaded generation.

Hugs,

Paul & Gretel

Precious Lord Jesus,
I ask that You be with me in a very real way,
not only when I must endure
suffering and humiliation,
but also when I am enjoying success
and Your anointing.
May I never forget
that I am first and foremost Your servant.
Help me to humbly serve others
in such a way as to never cause offense to You
or discredit Your precious name.
Amen.

Chapter 6

UNSHAKEABLE ASSURANCE

Dearly Beloved,

"Nevertheless,
the firm foundation of God stands . . ."
(2 Timothy 2:19)

The Lord impressed this verse upon us one morning with such an unmistakable and powerful anointing that it made us draw in our breath sharply with excitement. It was as if we'd never really heard what the Holy Spirit was saying before. We repeated that phrase with a special emphasis first on the word **"Nevertheless,"** then on the words **"firm foundation of God,"** and then, finally and triumphantly, on the word **"stands."** We knew that we had been given a gift of faith to believe in the divine truthfulness of this verse.

We felt the force of God's love and concern for His people and for us especially, as surely as if He had physically put His arms around us. We experienced the unshakable assurance from on high that no matter what happened, we were to remember this moment and this undeniable truth. It was indelibly engraved upon our minds and hearts with the branding iron of His love. It has become a powerful weapon against disappointment, fear, anger, shock, "poor-me-ism," and a host of other tools of the enemy that had been used against us.

Right after receiving this Word, we suffered a stunning blow to our personal finances when the company whose sporting goods catalog Paul's "tent-making" marketing partnership had published for two years decided not to renew their account. Suddenly we realized that we were not "blown away" by this financial reverse because we knew with a certainty that: **"Nevertheless, the firm foundation of God stands."** Hope and peace did not leave us for a second because He had girded us with this truth.

We could even chuckle when our cold water faucet froze in the bathtub in a siege of –12°F. temperature, because we recognized that it was just another attempt of the enemy to discourage us. Reminding each other that **"Nevertheless, the firm foundation of God stands,"** we calmly thawed the pipe with no sense of panic (an electric hair dryer is a wonderful invention!) And there were no leaks—PTL!

Now, when we hear a report about a Christian whose gross sin is trumpeted in the the media, we remind ourselves of the rest of this verse, **"Nevertheless, the firm foundation of God stands, having this seal, 'The Lord knows those who are His' . . ."** We are not to be vexed about whether that person is really a Christian or not. God is very well aware of **"those who are His"** and they will receive their just reward from Him. He expects us to treat everyone with love and respect, and understanding this Scripture helps us to do it.

Our verse ends by declaring **" . . . 'Let every one who names the name of the Lord abstain from wickedness.' "** We who **"name the name of the Lord"** are expected by God, our fellow Christians, and even our unbelieving family and friends, to **"abstain from wickedness."** There are no extenuating circumstances mentioned in the Bible that excuse a Christian for acting wickedly. Lest we forget, the word wicked means "morally very bad; evil ... disposed to mischief ... disgustingly unpleasant ... causing or likely to cause harm, distress, or trouble." Our lives must show that we rejoice in the truth that **"Righteousness and justice are the foundation of Thy throne . . ."** (Psalm 89:14) and should be the foundation of our lives.

We heard the news of the horrendous earthquake in the San Fernando Valley, California, before the news hit the airwaves. Our daughter received an early morning telephone call from a prayer partner. Alexis and her family lived, worked, and pastored in the Valley for ten years and have many dear friends living there. Her terrified friend, calling for prayer, reported that she and her family were unhurt and their house was still standing, but every thing in it was jumbled and they were without power and water. The frightening after-shocks were still rumbling, but they were alive and thanking God for His mercy. Alexis immediately began to pray for them. Using this promise: **"Nevertheless, the firm foundation of God stands!"**, she exhorted them to remember that He is Lord, eternal, and unshakable, and we who live in Him need not tremble or be afraid.

During the next few days, as we watched the television, we were appalled by the extent and the depth of the devastation which happened in a twinkling of an eye. The lives that were lost, the family pictures, the treasured gifts, the favorite hairbrush, the collection of records, the hand-written recipes, the love letters, and the books and paintings and furniture—all gone and all irreplaceable! There is much grieving that must be allowed to be expressed under the watchful eye of the Holy Spirit.

We reject that old religious "knee-jerk" reaction that immediately says, "Another catastrophe for California. God is punishing them for their sins. Now maybe they will repent." Christians should know better than to proclaim that this was an "act of God." It is a cruel and unthinking judgment and plays right into Satan's plans to have us blame God for all disasters.

If God wanted to get the attention of those with whom He really was angry enough to destroy, He could have had the earth swallow up only the adult bookstores; the gang headquarters; the gay communities; the abortion clinics; the houses of prostitutes and pimps; the casinos; the dishonest businesses; the porno movie and video studios; the drug houses; the cult leaders' homes; and the homes of all who are wicked; and leave the righteous unharmed. This did not happen!

Neither sin nor natural catastrophe has the power to dislodge the firm foundation of God. Knowing this, we can stand and persevere in any circumstance with our feet firmly planted on the unshakeable Rock of Jesus.

Hugs,

Paul & Gretel

Lord Jesus, You are our rock,
the very foundation of our lives.
We confess that there are times
when we wobble in our confidence that Your truth
can stand the onslaughts of the world's wickedness
and the enemy's lies.
Forgive us, Lord, when we are shaky and weak.
Renew our confidence in Your steadfastness,
Lord Jesus,
and our sure knowledge that—
regardless, no matter what, and nevertheless—
"the firm foundation of God stands!"
Amen.

Chapter 7

PRAYING GOD'S HEART

Dearly Beloved,

**"For we also once were foolish ourselves,
disobedient, deceived, enslaved to
various lusts and pleasures,
spending our life in malice and envy, hateful,
hating one another.
But when the kindness of God our Savior and
His love for mankind appeared,
He saved us,
not on the basis of deeds
which we have done in righteousness,
but according to His mercy,
by the washing of regeneration and
renewing by the Holy Spirit,
whom He poured out upon us richly
through Jesus Christ our Savior . . ."**
(Titus 3:3–6)

We continue to be amazed to hear how some sincere Christians are fervently praying for God to allow disaster to break into sinners' lives in order to force them into accepting Jesus as a last resort. They pray as if God designed calamities to be used as an evangelistic tool. The Apostle Paul was convinced that it is the kindness and the love of God for humans, even in their sin, that draws them to Him. What a picture these misguided Christians must have of a revengeful God sitting up in heaven plotting and executing ways to destroy His children's health, finances, or personal relationships and then expecting those battered children to turn to Him and give Him their trusting love.

These kinds of prayers are prayers of the flesh which are received by Satan as an invitation to wreak havoc in someone's life—not to give them a push toward God, but rather a shove into the pit of despair and hopelessness!

If this theory of making people turn to God because of tragedy were true, God would certainly withhold any blessings from the sinner, yet Jesus is recorded in Matthew 5:45 as saying, "**. . . He causes His sun to rise on the evil and the good, and sends rain on the righteous and the unrighteous.**" Our problem is that WE don't know who will eventually respond to God's wooing! God knows, and yet He continues to allow us all the freedom to live under His grace with the tares among the wheat. But unlike those tares in Jesus' parables, there is a miracle waiting for us that will turn us useless weeds into fruitful wheat. Being reborn should be that much of a contrast to our old self as we die to our will and are resurrected a new creature in Him.

The passage from Titus reminds us that in our own way we were as sinful as the ones for whom we are praying, yet He loved us enough not to wipe us out, patiently giving us every opportunity to recognize Him as the author of our existence. It was His love and kindness towards us that melted our hearts. It is when we sinners receive this gift of revelation that we really become aware of our sinful ways and how much we need a savior. Our hearts are overwhelmed that He is willing to love us despite our past, and we find ourselves begging Him to forgive us and inviting Him to enter in and become Lord of our lives.

Who are we Christians to judge that a sinner needs an object lesson of calamity to jar him or her into the

Kingdom? Romans 2:4 warns us not to judge others thus: **"Or do you think lightly of the riches of His kindness and forbearance and patience, not knowing that the kindness of God leads you to repentance?"**

A few years ago we were in a prayer meeting with precious Christians who had been misled into thinking that the best way for the nation of England to be brought to its knees in repentance was to pray for the bottom to drop out of its economic system so that people would have no other place to turn but to God! When we protested that they were unwittingly inviting more than they could ever bargain for, they were surprised. We asked them, "What will you do when you lose your jobs and your parents have no income from their pensions?"

It is easier to say, "Go punish the greedy, Lord!" than it is to experience our own nation's financial base disintegrate along with our livelihood and our ability to help others in need. If what was being "prayed" ever happened, no business or government could afford to support anyone. God is not obligated to support us during our hardships when we are wishing hardship on others.

Our observation has been that people often become so embittered when they have lost the ability to feed, house, and clothe their families through no fault of their own, that they harden their hearts against a God who they think would allow such suffering.

Shortly after this experience, the Lord gently reprimanded us for preparing to pray, "God, cause our [prodigal] son to fail in everything he does until he finally cries out to you in mercy and comes back to you." Instead, He instructed us to ask Him in faith to bless him that he might come to know His kindness and love towards him even while he was a sinner. As we prayed blessings upon him, ***our*** hearts began to change; a deeper love began to flow toward him that drew him back to us. We realized that he had sensed he was hopeless in our eyes.

Our testimony is that God has indeed showered His blessings upon him, giving him favor with his employer and the courage to make more righteous decisions. We have noticed that he is much more open to recognizing that it is not his luck but rather God's blessing. Our son has been visibly touched by the Lord's unfailing love and His willingness not to give up on him.

Now, when people ask us how he is, we just smile and say: "He is building his testimony!"

Just recently we were talking with a couple whose unsaved father's business was at the point of bankruptcy. They were praying that this humiliation and stripping of what they judged to be his idol and identity would bring him to his knees. "What about his employees?" we asked. "What about the people who own and work for the companies who will be devastated financially because he can't pay them for their services or products? What about the rest of your family who will suffer with him? Will they be praising God? If he is embittered, won't he be less likely to turn to God with hope?"

"Start praying for a financial miracle to save that company and all those who would be adversely affected by its demise and bankruptcy. Be bold and tell your dad how you are praying to your God. Then pray and watch God work!" They did, and He did! Praise the Lord!

We Christians need to be praying for the economic health of our countries—in fact for the whole world—so that people might have the dignity returned to them of being able to support their families in an honorable way and be able to care for the afflicted with offerings and alms.

Hugs,

Paul & Gretel

Dear Father,
so often I find myself praying corrective prayers,
or prayers of lament,
instead of the kindly prayers of Your heart.
Forgive me my judgmental attitudes,
and let me remember
Your many kindnesses to me so that I might be
as lavish with my kindness to others as
You have been with me.
Amen.

Chapter 8

DIGNITY IN DIFFICULTY

Dearly Beloved,

"... in all things show yourself
to be an example of good deeds,
with purity in doctrine, dignified,
sound in speech which is beyond reproach,
in order that the opponent may be put to shame,
having nothing bad to say about us."
(Titus 2:7–8)

In his pastoral letters to Timothy and Titus, the Apostle Paul offered them sound, practical, and divine advice for wrestling with problems, challenges, and difficult situations that they had never faced before. As we dwelt in these love letters to his beloved children in the Lord, we noticed how strongly he exhorted them to display DIGNITY in DIFFICULTY.

Dignity may seem to be an odd word for the "swinging nineties," but if the Apostle Paul thought it to be a vital qualification for leadership and a distinguishing trait for the whole Body of Christ, we had better ponder its definition and its application to our lives.

According to *The American Heritage Dictionary*, dignity is "The presence of poise and self-respect in one's deportment to a degree that inspires respect; inherent nobility and worth."

That Paul would list dignity as a leadership quality should not be surprising as Jacob, inspired by the Holy Spirit, prophetically blessed his first-born son, Reuben, as going to be **"preeminent in dignity"** (Genesis 49:3).

The writer of Proverbs described the "**excellent wife**" (perhaps connoting the Bride of Christ) as being clothed with "**strength and dignity**" (Proverbs 31:25).

Even though we do not seem to see much of this kind of real dignity modeled for us these days by celebrities, politicians, or even church superstars, it remains a valid biblical qualification for leadership in the Body of Christ.

- "**He** (an "overseer" in the church) **must be one who manages his own household well, keeping his children under control with all dignity.**" (1 Timothy 3:4)
- "**Deacons likewise must be men of dignity...**" (1 Timothy 3:8)
- "**Women must likewise be dignified...**" (1 Timothy 3:11)
- "**Older men are to be temperate, dignified, sensible, sound in faith, in love, in perseverance.**" (Titus 2:2)

The Apostle Paul even declares dignity to be one of the primary objectives of our prayer life for the world and society in which we live: "**First of all, then, I urge that entreaties and prayers, petitions and thanksgivings, be made on behalf of all men, for kings and all who are in authority, in order that we may lead a tranquil and quiet life in all godliness and dignity.**" (1 Timothy 2:1–2)

It has occurred to us, as we review these emphases on dignified behavior in the early Church, that dignity might well be one of the God-ordained separators between the Christian and the heathen world systems. In order for that to be true in reality, however, we Christians need to start modeling true dignity to the world by our words and actions.

Perhaps we have been concentrating so much on our doctrinal purity that we have neglected the basics of dignity and sound speech beyond reproach. Perhaps we have allowed our zeal to save the lost to quench our sensitivity to how we look and sound to them even as we try to reach them.

For example, we observed a street preacher in Wales ranting over a hand-held loudspeaker about the evils of TV, the degraded morals of the youth, and the wrath which God was about to pour forth on Great Britain if the people did not all repent ***now***. We witnessed the disgust, yes and even rancor, he stirred up in the people who were forced to hear him as they quietly went about their Saturday morning business in the town center.

Surely Jesus, who is our perfect model for all our behavior, conducted Himself with unpretentious natural dignity at all times. And we are currently hearing accounts of the incredible dignity with which our brothers and sisters in the persecuted church around the world are facing unthinkable treatment and even death.

We offer you a challenge: let the Spirit of the Lord Jesus work ***His*** dignity into your life so that you, in all of your behavior, will inspire respect, honor, and esteem in all those who observe you.

In all things, let us show ourselves to be an example of dignity, beyond reproach, in order that any opponent may be put to shame, having nothing bad to say about us.

Hugs,

Paul & Gretel

Heavenly Father, I confess that I don't feel that I even
begin to understand how to act dignified,
especially in difficult situations.
But I desire to,
so that I can exhibit You
and Your Son Jesus at all times!
Help me, oh Lord,
to refrain from "losing my cool" and acting
undignified or unbecomingly—
at least I know what they mean.
Help me not to allow my mouth to convict me
in the court of my enemies.
May only sweet water flow from this well,
so that nothing bad can be said of You
because of what I do or say
that is not dignified.
Amen.

Chapter 9

POLITE AND PLEASANT UNDER PRESSURE

Dearly Beloved,

**"Keep your behavior excellent among the Gentiles,
so that in the thing in which
they slander you as evildoers,
they may on account of your good deeds,
as they observe them,
glorify God in the day of visitation."**
(1 Peter 2:12)

In this letter, we are continuing the theme of Christ-like behavior in crisis situations with a fresh perspective of how important it is that our behavior always be polite and pleasant under pressure.

Problems are apt to bring to the surface perversity instead of polite perseverance in times of pressure. This perverse tendency to not act with politeness and pleasantness under pressure springs from the unredeemed areas of our hearts, and can, by its lack of consideration for others, wreak havoc in the lives of the very people that God has put us among to model the character of His Son. God has purposed that our Godly behavior in crunch times shows the people of the world that we Christians ***are*** different, and that the difference is admirable and desirable.

Unfortunately, it is not uncommon for otherwise commendable believers to exhibit unsanctified behavior under pressure. Many years ago, a well-known writer and conference speaker accepted our invitation to minister to some business leaders and their wives at a dinner party in our home on the night prior to a major conference. His baggage did not arrive with him—a not unusual experience for one who travels a great deal! At the baggage claim counter, to our shock and great embarrassment, he berated the harried agent with the harshest outburst of language we have ever heard that did not include profanity.

All the agent could do was to apologize and assure him that they would get his bags to him at his hotel as soon as possible. But that was not enough for our "important" guest who proceeded to tell the poor lad how famous he was, and if he did not have his suitcase by 5 p.m. he would see that the airline's president (whom he knew personally) heard about the incident, and that would not help the agent's job security.

We have often wondered what would have happened if that clerk had been a seeker who went to the conference the next day to hear "the man of God" and recognized him as the person who had so unfairly scalded him with his tongue for something over which he had absolutely no control!

We realized that our guest speaker's mind-set at that moment was totally focused on himself and on his problem; in other words, on the things of the flesh. Out of the limelight, he had reverted to the authoritarian demeanor of the "old" man still in him. This experience shocked us, but God graced us with this admonition: **"For those who are according to the flesh set their minds on the things of the flesh, but those who are according to the Spirit, the things of the Spirit. For the mind set on the flesh is death, but the mind set on the Spirit is life and peace."** (Romans 8:5–6)

That "death" can be death to those innocents around us!

This incident so affected us as young Christians that we knelt together at the foot of our bed that night and cried out to God to forgive that leader, to convict him of his behavior, and to comfort the abused airline employee. Then, we asked God to never let us forget the lesson that outburst of rudeness taught us, and keep us from ever being impolite to anyone no matter what their position, gender, age, wealth, race, or health, even when we are under pressure.

It is so easy to overlook someone when we are in a hurry, or stressed by frustration, anger, self-pity, or fatigue. To show our impatience with another's slowness, ineptitude, immaturity, or lack of ability to solve our immediate problem is simply immature self-centeredness ... that's the mind set on the flesh!

Respect and kindness were some of Jesus' character traits that endeared Him to the ordinary people. Jesus treated the woman at the well with polite respect as He listened to her and conversed with her. He was pleasant and loving to the little children who played at His feet. He did not accuse the tax collector, Zaccheus, of being dishonest, but rather, politely asked to have lunch in his home. That changed Zaccheus' life forever. He did not treat Mary Magdalene rudely because of her reputation. His uncondemning love toward her shocked His straight-laced host, but won her heart! He did not snarl at the soldiers who beat Him and nailed Him to the cross. Rather, He asked His Father God to forgive them just before He breathed His last. **"Now when the centurion saw what had happened, he began praising God, saying, 'Certainly this man was righteous.'"** (Luke 23:47) Jesus' behavior under extreme pressure was the witness that opened that soldier's heart to believe the Christ on the cross.

The Apostle Paul wrote to the Corinthian Church: **"He made Him who knew no sin to be sin on our behalf, that we might become the righteousness of God in Him. And working together with Him, we also urge you not to receive the grace of God in vain ... giving no cause for offense in anything, in order that the ministry be not discredited..."** (2 Corinthians 5:21–6:1 & 3)

Do you think for a moment that Joseph was rude and unpleasant while he earned his rank of head slave and overseer of Potiphar's house? We must ask our God, Joseph's God, to give us the same anointing in whatever pressure cooker we are in. And in the Name of Jesus, He will do it for us just as surely as He did it for Joseph!

It is God's grace that changes our nature so that we respond His way. The fruit of the Holy Spirit (Galatians 5:22–23) includes peace, patience, kindness, goodness, gentleness, and self-control; all of which are listed as synonyms for politeness in the thesaurus. We are designed to cooperate with the Holy Spirit, to listen carefully to His instructions, and to allow Him to teach us and to guide our actions into harmony with Jesus.

Hugs,

Paul & Gretel

Lord Jesus, sometimes it is really hard
not to react to other people's rudeness.
But I guess I don't have to tell You that.
I am in awe of how gently You handled the sinners
and how firmly You confronted the religious.
Your spirit was never condescending or vicious.
Your words and actions were designed to woo and
convict those who needed to be saved.
May people never again observe me
as I once was before You changed my heart.
May others give You praise as they see what only You
could have possibly accomplished in me!
Amen.

Chapter 10

KEEP YOUR PUPPY LOVE

Dearly Beloved,

"But I have this against you, that you have left your first love."
(Revelation 2:4)

We are in awe over the variety of ways God chooses to get our attention, and to direct us onto new paths. Some are so subtle that we are not really aware that He has led us to change our mindset or heart attitude until others comment on the difference they observe in our actions. Other times, He orchestrates major upheavals that startle us into recognizing His intentions. Let us explain what happened to us to better illustrate our point.

It was on the morning of Christmas Eve that we looked out and saw a half-grown, half-starved black Labrador retriever moping around the barns. We phoned around to inquire about any missing dog with no success. We did not feed him lest he attach himself to us—our hearts were still very tender from having lost our yellow Lab, Chuckles, a year ago and we had decided not to get another dog. We assumed that the lost dog would find his way home eventually.

A week later, we discovered the now emaciated creature huddled in a ball at our back gate shivering in the sub-zero temperature. We both leapt out with water and food reminding ourselves all the while that we mustn't "get involved!" He bolted down two big bowls of food and drank and drank and leaned against us imploring us with soulful eyes. We were hooked! We advertised his "lostness" over the radio and then finally took him to the vet. "He is a thoroughbred Labrador, about a year old, starved of course, but he will be fine."

No one ever called to claim him, and God chuckled!

Having a bouncy, irrepressible dog of a large size changed our lives—again. Charlie insists on constant affection and has attached himself to our knees. He sleeps in our bedroom, lies on the bathroom rug (and we have a very small bathroom!), curls up under the table as we eat, and stretches out at our feet in the living room; alert to our every move. We trip over him as we dart back and forth from house to office and from room to room. We swear that we are developing calluses from having to pet him all the time.

Our "elder brother" office-cat, Marmalade, is not pleased, but Charlie is determined to win him over as well. (We have reminded Marmie, that he, too, was a starved, half-grown castaway who came out of the woods looking for a home and family and we took him into our hearts.)

Why do we say that we think God has arranged all of this? Not only to fill the empty part of our hearts and lives that Chuckles occupied for 13 years giving us such pleasure, but to rock us out of our settled ways and to teach us new lessons. God can teach "old dogs" new tricks—we're proof!

In our quiet time one morning, the Spirit of God sweetly spoke to us:

"Look at that dog, My children, really observe him. He is full of life and so grateful for your love and his rescue that he wants to be with you and please you at all times. When you first were fully adopted into My

kingdom, you were the same way; you wanted to be with Me day and night. You couldn't take your eyes off of Me. I've missed your unbounded enthusiasm and insistence on pressing into Me to learn what I wanted you to do next. You have opted to stroll these past few years where once you strained at the leash! Let this season of training Charlie show you where you once were and how I trained you. I didn't 'put out the fire,' but directed it to bring My light and My love to My children. You have plenty of fire left in you!

"I loved your eagerness to please. You were partly trained and housebroken, but let's face it, you too were prone to throw yourself at everything that moved and run away with it. You'd sit at My command, even if somewhat reluctantly, but were feverishly ready to spring into action at the slightest indication that there was action to get into. But when I said, 'Lie down!' I discovered that that wasn't one of the 'tricks' in your repertoire yet.

"You too would wolf down everything that looked liked food without checking or chewing, and consequently, had to vomit up some strange stuff! But you survived and didn't give up eating. Yes, you dug up some seeds and bulbs in My garden, as well, and had to be reprimanded. You, too, would leap up on everybody who crossed your path, and in your exuberance knocked down a few sedate and unprepared people.

"Through these years, you have learned obedience—through suffering. Suffering the loss of your own willful ways, and by being restrained by Me to keep you from rushing headlong into real trouble in your passion to charge ahead, even without My direction.

"You have learned through love and discipline. So will he. Be patient.

"Sometimes your feelings were hurt and you held back and you pouted a bit because you didn't see things quite the way I do, but in the end you opted to come under My authority. You could not stand being separated from Me by your sin! A child and a puppy both need to grow up to be useful, but an undisciplined child or puppy grows up to be a nuisance and a 'pain in the neck' to those around them, especially their master.

"Unbridled fervor turns into belligerent fanaticism which hardens hearts.

"Your generation needs the vivacity of youth around you: their sharp eyes, their keen ears, and their innocent and insatiable curiosity, to stir your ardor and spur you on to 'finish the course.' Take Charlie, and some of My young saints, on those long walks through the woods, down in the valleys, and up on the rocky cliffs like you used to do, and teach them the 'ropes.' You are too young, in My plan, to be 'put out to pasture!' Besides, the young need the seasoned experience, wisdom, and knowledge of those of you who have traveled My highway with Me for many years and learned of Me. I want you to guide them with love and encouragement, not sit back and squelch them with constant correction or criticism.

"Enjoy them, laugh with them, exhort them, wonder with them, cry with them, and rejoice with them, but don't envy them. Instead, revel in your knowledge of Me that you have acquired by years of close association with Me and share this relationship with others."

We share these personal words of blessing and encouragement with you in the hope that they will help you to better understand the heart of God for His people, both young and old.

Hugs,

Paul & Gretel

Heavenly Father, I love You!
I want to please You with my love the same way
this precious puppy pleases me with his.
Sometimes I get very conscious
that I too was a stray that You saved,
and I feel very unworthy of being in Your presence.
But that is where I long to be!
Forgive me for letting there be
any distance between us.
Help me too Lord to observe
and learn from the mature saints
with which You have graced my life.
Amen.

Chapter 11

PATIENCE

Dearly Beloved,

"... the fruit of the Spirit is
love, joy, peace, patience ..."
(Galatians 5:22)

Patience: *the capacity of calm endurance and tolerant understanding*

"Love is patient ..."
(1 Corinthians 13:4)

Patient: *bearing affliction with calmness or without complaint; manifesting forbearance or restraint under provocation or strain; bearing delay and waiting for the right moment—not hasty or impetuous—being steadfast despite opposition, difficulty, or adversity*

Patience is a virtue we all long to have but hate to spend the time and the effort to acquire!

It wasn't too many years ago that as we expressed our frustration about waiting for certain prayers to be answered, the Holy Spirit quietly told us,

"To hurry God is to find fault with Him!"

What a firm, but gentle, rebuke! We were immediately convicted of our faithless impatience which was focused on our idea of how things and people were to be, instead of on God's faithfulness. We had forgotten that the Lord had pointed out to us that: *"My plan is so much more encompassing and eternal than your finite minds can comprehend. And remember, I look at results differently than you do!"*

He brought us to Romans 9:22 to illustrate the

far-reaching intent of His redemption. Read it carefully, because it is hard to understand, and it is a verse we tend to "bump" over. **"What if God, although willing to demonstrate His wrath and to make His power known, endured with much patience vessels of wrath prepared for destruction?"**

"Why wait, God? Why not annihilate the 'baddies' right now in a show of Your power that would make the whole world tremble?"

His reply is the same as Jesus' was to James and John when they begged to be allowed to send fire down upon the inhospitable Samaritans: **"You do not know what kind of spirit you are of. For the Son of Man did not come to destroy men's lives, but to save them."** (Luke 9:55–56)

He then lovingly explained His strategy of patience as it is stated in the next verse (Romans 9:23): **"And He did so in order that He might make known the riches of His glory upon vessels of mercy, which He prepared beforehand for glory . . ."**

God used the sin of Pharaoh to develop Moses and prepare His people to leave their familiar life in Egypt and plunge into the desert. What Satan meant for evil, God patiently turned to good to bring His chosen people into the promised land.

Joseph learned to patiently trust His God through horrific injustices and saw the fulfillment of his prophetic dreams.

David was patient in his waiting to receive the kingdom because he trusted God to bring it to pass despite the bleakness of his situation. God patiently allowed King Saul time to repent!

The character of Jesus Christ is formed in us as we patiently yield to His will, His way, and His timetable. All of heaven is cheering us on to persevere through the rough times, to respond to adversity with God's love and forbearance, and to patiently wait for God's glory to burst through the darkness.

God wants us, by an act of our own free will, to learn to "**put on a heart of . . . patience**" (Colossians 3:12) so that we can "**. . . walk in a manner worthy of the calling with which** (we) **have been called, with all humility and gentleness, with patience showing forbearance to one another in love . . .**" (Ephesians 4:1–2)

The Apostle Paul entreats us to "**admonish the unruly, encourage the fainthearted, help the weak,** (and) **be patient with all men.**" (1 Thessalonians 5:14) He confesses, "**. . . I found mercy, in order that in me as the foremost** (sinner), **Jesus Christ might demonstrate His perfect patience, as an example for those who would believe in Him for eternal life.**" (1 Timothy 1:16)

This impetuous man had finally learned to patiently allow God to have His way in and through his life. His words to Timothy were to "**. . . preach the word . . . reprove, rebuke, exhort, with great patience and instruction.**" (2 Timothy 4:1–2)

The Apostle Paul wanted everyone to understand the "otherwiseness" of Jesus Christ who was the exact image of His Father. He warned the Roman Christians not to pass hasty judgments on one another as if God wasn't aware of their behavior. "**Or do you think lightly of the riches of His kindness and forbearance and patience, not knowing that the kindness of God leads you to repentance?**" (Romans 2:4)

Sometimes God uses the natural world to show us His nature. We watched with astonishment the patience with which our big black Labrador retriever, Charlie, allowed our 18-month-old grandson, Paul, to climb all over him and love him with clumsy hands and feet. Little Paul would crow with delight the minute Charlie entered the room and as Charlie would lie down patiently on his side, little Paul would rush to sit down next to him and lean against him and hug and tug and pull on him. Charlie endured the indignities without complaint, and trusted us to protect him from real harm, which we did as gently as possible when necessary.

When I was a little girl, I was allowed to go to my grandparents' summer home on a big lake in northern Minnesota. My grandfather plowed a garden for me and helped me sow potato eyes, which I zealously cultivated. As the potato leaves began to stretch toward the sun, I eagerly dug their roots up every morning to see how big the potatoes were. I had the tallest and lushest plants in the whole area, but ended up with only pea-sized potatoes, because in my impatience, I wouldn't leave them alone long enough to grow—I just had to uncover them to peek at their progress! I've never forgotten the disappointment, and the lesson my grandfather allowed me to learn about patience.

There is a wonderful thrill to see the fulfillment of patience. It takes time for people and plans (and potatoes!) to mature—don't hurry them. As we patiently endure setbacks and disappointments, periods of dryness and near-despair, pain and powerlessness, and yet keep on persevering in our walk with the Lord, we shall share in the riches of His glory.

Hugs,

Paul & Gretel

Patient Heavenly Father,
I thank You for Your lovingkindness
towards me all these years
when I have not always been
particularly patient with others
or, to my shame, even with You.
Forgive me for not trusting You to know best
the timing that will bring about
Your desired results in my life,
and in the lives of those I love.
Develop in me
true and divine "potato-patience," I pray.
Amen.

Chapter 12

WHAT CONCERN IS IT OF YOURS?

Dearly Beloved,

"...Lord, what about this man?'
Jesus said to him, ... 'What is that to you?
You follow Me!'"
(John 21:21–22)

This exchange between the reborn Apostle Peter and his beloved and resurrected Lord Jesus, articulates one of the biggest challenges we are experiencing in the church today. It also presents the clearest of instructions for overcoming that challenge with righteousness. Peter was expressing a concern for what lay ahead for the Apostle John. They were close friends, they had been together with Jesus for over three years, they had seen the empty grave together, they had touched the resurrected Christ, and Jesus had just told Peter his future. Peter was wondering what his friend John's future was to be.

Jesus' answer was very strong! A paraphrase might read: "Peter, I want you to put all your heart, soul, mind, and strength into following after Me. Even if I do something 'far out' with John—like letting him remain until I return—what concern is it of yours? You follow Me!"

We believe that after this heart-to-heart exchange with Jesus, every time thoughts came to Peter about the position, walk, or practices of another servant of God, Peter re-heard Jesus' words blazing in his heart: **"...What is that to you? You follow Me!"** and kept his mind and his mouth off his brothers and sisters.

This is perhaps one of the reasons the Holy Spirit could release so much through the Apostle Peter. We say this because Revelation 12:10 says: "**And I heard a loud voice in heaven, saying, 'Now the salvation, and the power, and the kingdom of our God and the authority of His Christ have come, for the accuser of our brethren has been thrown down, who accuses them before our God day and night.'**" Think about it! Salvation and power, the Kingdom of God, and the authority of Christ come because the accuser of the brethren is thrown down.

We submit to you on the basis of these Scriptures, that we all should change our present ways of praying for revival, to praying for the pulling down of the stronghold of the accuser of the brethren: first of all in ourselves, and then in the whole Body of Christ! Will we not then experience a new flow of salvation and power, a new reality to Kingdom life, and a new dimension to the authority of Christ in the disciples of Christ? These things, after all, are the key facets to what most of us mean when we cry for revival!

In John 3:17 Jesus speaks strongly to us about His role while He was here on earth: "**For God did not send the Son into the world to judge the world; but that the world should be saved through Him.**" Jesus picks up on this theme as He addresses the Pharisees in John 8:15: "**You people judge according to the flesh; I am not judging any one.**" In John 20:21 Jesus says: "**. . . as the Father has sent Me, I also send you.**" Therefore, we are sent by our Lord Jesus to save, not to judge. And we are most definitely not to judge according to the flesh as the Pharisees were rebuked for doing. But neither are we to crush the Holy Spirit's gifts of discernment under a heap of guilt or fear of being used by the spirit of the accuser of the brethren!

Jesus said in John 7:24, **"Do not judge according to appearance, but judge with righteous judgment."** There is clearly a lawful and righteous judgment that flows from the Holy Spirit. We must learn to rightly discern the ideas and the spirit behind the actions of our brothers and sisters without judging the person and without assuming a motive. Otherwise, we can be led into accusing which causes division, dissension, and strife.

Hebrews 5:14 says, "**. . . solid food is for the mature, who because of practice have their senses trained to discern good and evil.**" Discerning means "to thoroughly and completely judge," so do not try to hide from this issue by saying: "I don't judge, I discern!"

Righteous judgment, or discernment, is a necessary skill for Kingdom living. We must train our senses to do it correctly by following the Holy Spirit's leading, or we will surely be drawn into the sin of accusing! To judge means: "to form an opinion through careful weighing of evidence and testing of premises." But to accuse means: "to charge with a fault or offense, to blame someone." The form that this sin takes in the Body of Christ today is finger pointing and blaming. It is anointed by the ungodly spirit of the accuser of the brethren to tear apart what God is building and to tear down those who God is building up. The accuser can only be defeated when we refuse him access to our minds or our mouths!

A good general guideline for judging righteously and avoiding being used by the accuser, is to judge only where we are willing to give our life for the one we judge. This was Jesus' standard! If we live by it, we will not find ourselves accusing each other. Rather, we will become healers and exhorters!

And remember, righteously judge the word, idea, or deed, but not the person—that role belongs solely to Jesus when He returns again!

Hugs,

Paul & Gretel

Heavenly Father,
I pray that I will learn to follow Your Holy Spirit
in judging righteously. Give me a spirit of discernment
and help me pull down the unholy spirit
of the accuser of the brethren
from my life, and bring forth
Your mighty revival, Lord!
Amen.

Chapter 13

BURIED OR PLANTED

Dearly Beloved,

"Truly, truly, I say to you,
unless a grain of wheat falls into the earth and dies,
it remains by itself alone; but if it dies,
it bears much fruit."
". . . what shall I say,
'Father, save Me from this hour?'
But for this purpose I came to this hour."
(John 12:24 & 27)

Each spring, Christians joyously celebrate the breaking of the tyranny of the prince of this world over us which took place almost 2,000 years ago—some call it Easter, but we prefer to call it Resurrection Day. We who were once slaves to sin have been set free and should be deliriously happy about it! To us, Resurrection Day is a triumph of good over evil, justice over injustice, freedom over slavery, light over darkness, and life over death. It commemorates our deliverance **"from the domain of darkness"** and our miraculous transference **"to the kingdom of His** (God's) **beloved Son, in whom we have redemption, the forgiveness of sins."** (Colossians 1:13–14) But even in our joy, we are soberly aware that it took Jesus' death to bring us eternal life, and we weep because of the pain He endured on our behalf.

Jesus was willing to offer Himself as the ransom for all of us who believe that He is the Son of God. Mind-boggling, isn't it!

And Satan was ecstatic—at first! At last he would see the end of his "rival"—he thought. But the "dead seed" of Jesus' buried body contained the "living seed" of Resurrection Life that responded to the Holy Spirit's call. When Jesus burst forth from His grave, the heavy load of sin that He carried onto the cross and into the grave was left behind Him, and an indestructible and glorified Jesus arose as Lord of all!

Hell shook, and Satan trembled and gnashed his teeth with frustration, failure, and fear.

There is a difference between our understanding of the words "bury" and "plant," even though both involve placing something in the earth. When we bury something, we usually want to dispose of it, and we expect it to decay and be forgotten. But when we plant something, we always expect that the living seed within the dead-looking outer husk will spring forth with fresh new life, begin to grow up and out of the confines of the earth into the light, and be energized to produce fruit.

Jesus knew when He bore the sins of the world, that when He carried them all to the grave, the Life in Him would burst through the corruption of sin and death into life eternal.

The Pharisees wanted Him buried in a tomb to decay and be forgotten, but God had a greater plan! He planted Jesus in the earth like a grain of wheat. As Jesus Himself said: "**. . . Unless a grain of wheat falls into the earth and dies, it remains by itself alone; but if it dies, it bears much fruit.**" (John 12:24) God knew that seeds from this fruit would in turn be planted, until "**the whole earth is full of His glory.**" (Isiaih 6:3) Left behind Jesus, still "buried" in the grave, were the sins of the world and their power to control future generations of His believers.

When we receive Christ, the seed of His life comes to dwell in us. **"Therefore we have been buried with Him through baptism into death, in order that as Christ was raised from the dead through the glory of the Father, so we too might walk in newness of life."** (Romans 6:4)

Satan had no idea when he crucified Jesus that God and His Son had predestined (decided before the worlds began) that each human being that became united with Jesus through faith would be crucified with Christ, buried with Him in baptism, and then raised up with Him to new life in Christ: **". . . our old self was crucified with Him, that our body of sin might be done away with, that we should no longer be slaves to sin; for he who has died is freed from sin."** Because of this miracle, we can **". . . consider yourselves** (ourselves) **to be dead to sin, but alive to God in Christ Jesus."** (Romans 6:6–7 & 11)

The literal translation of Romans 6:5 establishes this as God's perspective on our dying to sin and self: **"For if we have been planted together in the likeness of His death, we shall also be of His resurrection."** You are not just buried with Christ, you are planted with Him! And, if you pick up your cross daily, your life will bring forth the new seed of Christ's life in others.

Satan would love to have you believe that your debts (sins) are too many for Jesus' death to cancel; or that to die to sin and be planted is too painful for you to bear; or that your planting is just a burial—nothing will ever arise from your death to self.

Don't you believe it!

We were all born again—planted and resurrected with Him—to bear new fruit for the Glory of God the Father.

How about making every day Resurrection Day from now on!

Hugs,

Paul & Gretel

Heavenly Father, Take my life
and plant it deep in the soil of Jesus.
Water it with Your Holy Spirit
so that I will abundantly bring forth
the good fruit of righteousness
for Your glory.
Amen.

Chapter 14

HONESTLY DIFFERENT

Dearly Beloved,

"...as those who have been chosen of God, holy and beloved, put on (clothe yourself with) **a heart of *compassion*,** (an empathetic consideration, a sympathetic understanding)
***kindness*,** (the quality of being kind, tender, and courteous)
***humility*,** (the grace not to think too highly of ourselves)
***gentleness*,** (the trait of showing tenderness) **and *patience*;,** (the willingness to endure without complaint)
***bearing with one another*,** (the habit of supporting or lovingly tolerating) **and *forgiving each other*, whoever has a complaint against any one; just as the Lord forgave you, so also should you. And beyond all these things put on *love*, which is the perfect bond of unity. And let the *peace of Christ* rule in your hearts, ... and *be thankful*..."** (being grateful and satisfied)
(Colossians 3:12–15)

These verses from Colossians are an invitation for all of us to enter into a genuine and honest oneness with Jesus. As the visible witnesses of the Kingdom of God, we, the Church, must learn to unequivocally **"...consider the members of** [our] **earthly** [bodies] **as dead to immorality, impurity, passion, evil desire, and greed, which amounts to idolatry. For it is on**

account of these things that the wrath of God will come upon the sons of disobedience, and in them [we] **also once walked, when** [we] **were living in them."** (Colossians 3:5–7)

The Apostle Paul continues to entreat us as believers in Jesus Christ to "**...put them all aside: anger, wrath, malice, slander, and abusive speech from your mouth."** (verse 8) He is firmly exhorting us not to "**...lie to one another, since** [we] **laid aside the old self with its evil practices, and have put on** [clothed ourselves with] **the new self who is being renewed to a true knowledge according to the image of the One who created** [us]**...**" (verses 9–10).

If every evangelist would require each of their new converts to immediately lay aside the old evil practices by renouncing them vehemently and then, in faith, clothing themselves with Jesus as their acknowledged and trusted Redeemer, what a different kind of Church we would be. If we all wore His nature as a mantle of righteousness, what a different kind of witness we could present to the world. What a joy and encouragement we would be to one another!

The new babes in Christ should be exhorted to renew their minds on a daily basis. We can testify that this is an exhilarating and intimate bonding experience with the Holy Spirit. Remember, Jesus loves us just the way we are now, but He also loves us enough not to leave us this way!

These new converts (and us older ones, too!) need to be assured by the words and actions of our fellow-believers that we will be loved, forgiven, and accepted when we occasionally "miss the mark" as we learn the "**...distinction between the holy and the profane, and between the unclean and the clean."** (Leviticus 10:10)

To make an impact on the hearts of those who do not know the Lord, we Christians need to do more than just pass out tracts, march and sing rousing songs, and preach convicting passages from the Bible from the pulpit or from the curb! The Living God is transforming us into His image to be a living book that people can read. It is designed by God to contain essays of His love and purity, reality and hope, compassion and forgiveness that will become welcoming beacons to pierce the stormy darkness of this world and guide the helpless and lost to the safe haven of His Kingdom.

We have to be honestly different from sinners on a daily basis or we end up being a living lie to the efficacy of the Cross. We are not to act weirdly, but quietly, dependably, and righteously Christ-like! Who will want to know our God if we Christians think, speak, and act just like the people of the world?

If neither you nor your family can observe that your heart attitude and life has been changed demonstrably after a confession of belief in Jesus Christ, may we suggest that you return to God on your knees again, and ask Him for the gift of repentance and a Godly sorrow for your past sins. Acknowledge that you have sinned against Him and others, and publicly abdicate your position as king on the throne of your life.

Now it is time to humbly invite the Lord Jesus to take His rightful place on the throne of your life. When you renounce past habits and practices and clothe yourself with your Lord, Jesus Christ, you will experience a genuine change of heart and mind that will be obvious to all. There will no longer be any need for pretending!

The angels in heaven will dance and celebrate, and Jesus will clap His hands with joy over being given another precious gift (you) for the Kingdom of His Father!

Hugs,

Paul & Gretel

Lord Jesus, thank You for choosing me!
I want to be a pure and wholly holy gift to You
that will fill You with glee and make You proud
to present me to Your Father.
Clothe me with Yourself so completely
that it will be plain for all to see
that You are on the throne of my life.
Amen.

Chapter 15

CONSUMMATE, CALIBRATE, AND CELEBRATE

Dearly Beloved,

"For I am convinced that neither death, nor life, nor angels, nor principalities, nor things present, nor things to come, nor powers, nor height, nor depth, nor any other created thing, shall be able to separate us from the love of God, which is in Christ Jesus our Lord."
(Romans 8:38–39)

As we were sharing the Scriptures with each other, we sensed the Holy Spirit gently urging us to focus on three areas of our walk with Jesus during the coming months:

"Consummate your relationship with Jesus;
Calibrate your behavior by His example; and
Celebrate the truth of His Lordship in all things."

The Lord is leading us all to meditate on these words as they pertain to our relationship with Him.

Everywhere we travel, the saints express in amazingly similar terms that the Lord is calling them closer to Himself. This is currently a major emphasis of the Holy Spirit to the Body of Christ, the Church. We suspect that this has always been His desire, as witnessed by Mark 3:13–15: **"And He** (Jesus) **went up to the mountain and summoned those whom He Himself wanted, and they came to Him. And He appointed twelve, that they might be with Him, and that He might send them out to preach, and to have authority to cast out the demons."**

Jesus' top priority for His initial disciples was that they come to Him when He called them **"that they might be with Him."** This is still His top priority, and through the Holy Spirit's ministry, He is drawing us all to make it OUR top priority.

Consummate means "to sum up; to complete in every detail; to perfect or become perfected; to be extremely skilled and accomplished; to be of the highest degree; the ultimate end or finish." We are all being called away from religious busyness to consummate our personal relationship with our Lord Jesus to the fullest extent of these meanings of the word.

To use the word consummate in the marital sense (which is legitimate because we are the Bride of Christ), we are being called to ultimate intimacy with Jesus; and through Him, by the Holy Spirit, drawn closer and closer to our Heavenly Father God.

As an engineer, I (Paul) immediately related to the phrase "Calibrate your behavior by His example." *Calibrate* means "to standardize by determining the deviation from a standard so as to ascertain the proper correction factors; to establish a set of graduations to indicate values or positions." The concept intrigued me, and as I explained it to Gretel, we both became excited.

The definition of calibrate seems to completely fit the directions the pastoral epistles give for learning and practicing Christian behavior. The standard is Jesus. We determine the deviation, or how far away we are from His behavior, which is the only standard (not our own, or that of any man). And we do so in order to know how to correct our walk to more perfectly be identical to His.

As we mature and pass various of life's "examinations," we experience a series of "graduations" that indicate the Holy Spirit values that are worked into us and revealed through us by our increasingly Christ like behavior.

The word *celebrate* has a broad meaning of "to observe a notable occasion with special festivities." I think we all have special memories of past happy celebrations that bring us "warm fuzzy" feelings when we hear the word. But we think God is saying more to the Church about celebrating!

We are being exhorted to celebrate His Lordship even when the "notable occasion" is not a "warm fuzzy" situation! We are being called to initiate special festivities when situations are painful, unpleasant, beyond our control or our influencing, and happening increasingly because we are living in the midst of a dark and perverse generation!

We can celebrate the fact that God is on His throne, even though a dear friend has just lost the battle against cancer.

We can celebrate the fact that God is still in control, even when our children are going through the trauma of divorce, sickness, or financial disaster.

We can celebrate the fact that God is Almighty and that Jesus is Lord of all, even when many seem to totally ignore or even overtly oppose Them.

We can celebrate the fact that Jesus is the King of kings, even when so many of the world's industrial and political leaders seem corrupt, self-serving, insensitive to others, and impressed with their own power and dominion.

Beloved, this word to celebrate His Godship in all circumstances is more challenging than you may at first realize. We guarantee, as you meditate on this, you will be faced with the clear choice between lip service to the truth of God's omnipotence, or a real acceptance that He is God, and who God is!

This is His message to us: "I AM GOD!"

Of course you "believe" this, or you wouldn't even be reading this letter. But when you start getting real with God, you will find areas where you wonder if God is really God of all—or even God at all!

Beloved, He is! There is only one God, and He is calling us to establish this mindset now, during relatively minor turbulence in our lives, so that when the rains descend, and the floods come, and the winds blow, we will be able to stand in the midst of the whirlwind by the strength of His might, knowing that HE IS GOD!

So, Beloved, *"Consummate your relationship with Jesus; Calibrate your behavior by His example; and Celebrate the truth of His Lordship in all things."* Meditate on these things, and the God of peace will garrison and mount guard over your heart and your mind and bring you peace—in the midst of turmoil, trouble, or trial.

It is our fondest desire that you experience the fullness of His grace and peace each and every day of your walk with Him!

Hugs,

Paul & Gretel

Heavenly Father,
please grace my heart with a completeness
in my relationship with Your Son, my Lord Jesus;
please establish in me the standard of behavior
that Jesus set for us while He was here in
the flesh as we are; and please anoint me
to boldly celebrate the Lordship of Your Son Jesus
in all circumstances and all situations. Amen.

Chapter 16

PROCLAIM THE EXCELLENCIES OF CHRIST

Dearly Beloved,

"...you are a chosen race, a royal priesthood,
a holy nation,
a people for God's own possession,
that you may proclaim the excellencies of Him
who has called you out of darkness
into His marvelous light."
(1 Peter 2:9)

One of the ministries that we all have as disciples of Jesus Christ is to publicly make plain the excellency of our God. The Amplified version of this verse uses the words: **"that you may set forth the wonderful deeds and display the virtues and perfections of Him . . ."** We proclaim His excellency by displaying His virtues and perfections in our lives. **"For such is the will of God that by doing right you may silence the ignorance of foolish men."** (1 Peter 2:15)

According to the Apostle Peter, the very salvation of some people depends on their seeing Christ in you through your behavior: **"Keep your behavior excellent among the Gentiles, so that in the thing in which they slander you as evildoers, they may on account of your good deeds, as they observe them, glorify God in the day of visitation."** (1 Peter 2:12) There is only one way anyone is going to glorify God at His second coming: that is, if they have already received Him as the Christ which He proclaimed to be at His first coming. For when He comes again, He is coming in judgment!

The Apostle Paul's letter to Titus includes instructions on Christian behavior for him to give to believers so **"that they may adorn the doctrine of God our Savior in every respect."** (Titus 2:10) Did you ever dare to think of yourself as an adornment to the Gospel of Jesus Christ? The Apostle Paul says your life is an adornment to the Gospel when you behave like Jesus. What a blessing!

Both Peter and Paul emphasize that our behavior in the world will determine if some people become Christians or stay heathens. What a responsibility! And what a pleasure—to see saints walking worthy of their Lord Jesus because they saw Him in our lives! The Apostle Paul wrote in Colossians 2:5: **"...I am with you in spirit, rejoicing to see your good discipline and the stability of your faith in Christ."** Surely good discipline (especially discipline of self) and stability are much-needed character traits in all of us.

Please note that none of these verses indicate that the proclamation of the excellency of Christ Jesus is to be made just from a church pulpit! They all refer to the public declaration of Jesus by the life of the individual saint—that is, each one of us! And even more important, they pertain to our behavior out in the world where the sinners are, not just in a church sanctuary surrounded by other Christians.

We are increasingly counseling brothers and sisters in Christ who are being urged to leave their productive occupations in order to pursue "full-time" ministry. We write "full-time" in quotation marks because we firmly believe that everyone who confesses Jesus Christ as their Lord, is already automatically in full-time ministry! The only question is where that ministry is to operate. Is it in the world where the sinners are, or is it in the Body of Christ where the hurting, wounded, and recovering saints are, or is it in both?

Peter answers this question this way: **"Whoever speaks, let him speak, as it were, the utterances of God; whoever serves, let him do so as by the strength which God supplies; so that in all things God may be glorified through Jesus Christ, to whom belongs the glory and dominion forever and ever. Amen."** (1 Peter 4:11) Paul agrees with him as he writes to the Colossians: **"And whatever you do in word or deed, do all in the name of the Lord Jesus, giving thanks through Him to God the Father."** (Colossians 3:17) **"Whatever you do, do your work heartily, as for the Lord rather than for men; knowing that from the Lord you will receive the reward of the inheritance. It is the Lord Christ whom you serve."** (Colossians 3:23–24)

We want to share with you what we have shared with many others:

> *If the Lord has graced you with a productive job and given you the abilities needed to perform it well for the glory of God, be very cautious about leaving it and expecting the Body of Christ to support you as you minister! Be very sure that it is God who wants you to do so, not an over zealous kingdom-builder.*

We say this for four reasons. First, for the most part, the Body of Christ has not yet matured to the point of comprehending the actual costs of the ministry it receives. Therefore, there is seldom sufficient giving to adequately support ministries unless they resort to worldly fund-raising techniques, spiritual/financial cons, or misallocating funds (such as using tithes to build the temple instead of supporting the priests). It is also our opinion that the economic situation worldwide is going to make contributions increasingly hard to come by. Certainly we, and many ministries we are relating to, are already finding this to be the case. We are preaching "strip-down and disencumber" for the final push.

Second, the Lord is placing His people to be available for His special use when He pours out His power in revival. It is important that we do not move ourselves according to OUR plans before His purpose for us is fulfilled where He presently has us. It is a preemptive strike of the enemy to get us feeling restless or discouraged in our present place, so that we will move before God's plan unfolds for our full use for His glory where we are.

Third, the Lord Jesus wants His disciples in the world even though we are not to be part of it, for He prayed: **"I do not ask Thee** [Father] **to take them out of the world, but to keep them from the evil one."** (John 17:15)

Jesus called us to be the **"salt of the earth"** and the **"light of the world."** (Matthew 5:13–14) And the Apostle Paul also declared that we are to prove ourselves **"...blameless and innocent, children of God above reproach in the midst of a crooked and perverse generation, among whom you appear as lights in the world."** (Philippians 2:15) Beloved, the Church is getting quite good at beaming our light into dark places. But salt is only effective upon contact! We have to be there, to be in touch with people, to be salt for them!

Fourth, the Lord is bringing us new understanding of what the church should be and how He is constantly molding and forming the Body of Christ! If we give up our vocations right now to jump into ministries, we may well find ourselves locked into a dry, old wineskin before we even know what God's plans are for us!

Beloved, it is our prayer that you might stand firm where God has you right now, and every moment proclaim with your behavior the excellencies of your God "**. . . that you may stand perfect and fully assured in all the will of God.**" (Colossians 4:12)

Hugs,

Paul & Gretel

Holy Father,
Help me to stand where You have placed me.
I want to proclaim Your excellence
and the excellence of Your Son, our Lord Jesus,
with every breath I breath, with every word I speak,
and with every deed I do.
I pray that in all things in my life, You will be glorified
through Jesus Christ, to whom belongs all of the glory
and dominion and power forever and forever.
Amen.

Chapter 17

BE STEADFAST

Dearly Beloved,

"...we have not ceased to pray for you and to ask that you may be... strengthened with all power, according to His glorious might, for the attaining of all steadfastness and patience..."
(Colossians 1:9b & 11)

To be steadfast is to be faithful, constant, dedicated, dependable, enduring, spirited, unwavering, loyal, well-founded, and reliable.

In this time of instability in the world, we Christians must remain steadfast, not using incidences of terrorism, pressures of religious bigotry, or shifting political and economic systems as a reason to water down our faith or our commitment to be the light and life of Christ in this world. Sometimes that is a hard assignment, but if we determine to fulfill it in love, the Holy Spirit promises to be with us.

When the Apostle Paul heard of the **"love in the Spirit"** that the Colossians had, he addressed them as **"the saints and faithful brethren in Christ..."** (Colossians 1:2)

The power of the Holy Spirit is able to give us the strength to remain steadfast when things and people are being shaken all around us. Because of His might, we can be counted on to be there, solidly **"in Christ,"** when others are being **"tossed here and there by waves, and**

carried about by every wind of doctrine..." (Ephesians 4:14) We are not like "**the one who doubts** [who] **is like the surf of the sea driven and tossed by the wind ... being a double-minded man, unstable in all his ways**" (James 1:6 & 8), for verse 7 tells us "**...let not that man expect that he will receive anything from the Lord.**" How can God build character on a foundation laid on sand that shifts when the wind and the floods come?

In the agony of repentance, King David cried out: "**Create in me a clean heart, O God, and renew a steadfast spirit within me.**" (Psalm 51:10) He had lost that precious steadfastness that used to guard him against wavering in his love and awe of God. David knew that he desperately needed God's mercy to renew that steadfast spirit within him. His son, Solomon, wrote many years later that "**He who is steadfast in righteousness will attain to life...**" (Proverbs 11:19)

We Christians can be steadfast because of the sure knowledge of what Jesus accomplished on the cross for us. The Apostle Paul recalled the promises of Isaiah 25:8 and Hosea 13:14 when he wrote in 1 Corinthians 15:54b–55 "**Death is swallowed up in victory. O death, where is your victory? O death, where is your sting?**" and then he went on to explain in verses 56–58: "**The sting of death is sin, and the power of sin is the law; but thanks be to God, who gives us the victory through our Lord Jesus Christ. Therefore, my beloved brethren, be steadfast, immovable, always abounding in the work of the Lord, knowing that your toil is not in vain in the Lord.**"

The Apostle Paul was adamant about this victory as he exhorted the Romans: "**There is therefore now no condemnation for those who are in Christ Jesus. For**

the law of the Spirit of life in Christ Jesus has set you free from the law of sin and of death." (Romans 8:1–2)

We no longer need fear life or death because through Jesus our eternal life is assured and we know that He is with us supporting and strengthening us as we go about living the remaining days of our lives for His glory. Though none of us know the number of days we have left, we can live life to its fullness for we cannot be shaken from the truth—Truth lives within us! Therefore, we can be steadfast and patient even when our circumstances and all those around us seem to call for a compromise in our Christian moral standards or beliefs.

Mother Teresa was the featured speaker at the 1994 National Prayer Breakfast in Washington, D.C. She spoke eloquently on behalf of the unborn babies who are being deliberately killed because, as she explained, they would be too much trouble for their parents to raise for one reason or another. Author Philip Yancey wrote: "In her talk, she managed to reduce the abortion controversy to its simplest moral terms: life or death, love or rejection. 'Please, give me the child. I want it, I will care for it.' Already she has placed three thousand children with families in Calcutta."

President Clinton invited Yancey to ride back to the White House in the Presidential limousine for a personal interview. Yancey asked President Clinton, who is a confessed Christian, why he had shifted from his 1989 stand opposing abortion. We quote from the April 25th, 1994 issue of *Christianity Today*: "Clinton defends this shift by saying the approach to specific moral issues in a democracy should change as popular opinion changes."

What a shocking statement for a Christian to make! We share this about the president not to criticize, but to encourage you to pray for all those in authority to understand God's mandate to base our lives and morals on His Word, the Scriptures that President Clinton himself told Yancey he loves and reads daily, and not on popular opinions or public pluralities.

Despite the threats of losing their livelihoods, their homes, their families, or their lives, the early Christians remained steadfast to the truth. Their lives could have been so much easier had they just "gone along" with the Jewish religious system under the temple rule! Even some of their religious leaders recognized Jesus as a prophet, so why need they alienate the Pharisees by insisting that He was the Son of God?

Christians who live in Muslim countries today are being confronted by the very same argument. We were told by a devout Muslim that a whole chapter of the Koran is devoted to Jesus as a prophet. "If only you wouldn't insist that He rose from the dead or performed miracles—His teachings are good, why make Him out to be God? It separates us because that stand is offensive to us."

Pastor Mehdi Dibaj, a former Muslim, was imprisoned in Iran in 1983 for the crime of apostasy because 45 years ago he converted to Christianity and became a Christian minister. According to the April 1994 issue of *Renewal* magazine, "He was systematically tortured and suffered mock executions. He spent two years in solitary confinement in a dark cell three feet by three feet." When at last he was brought to trial before an Islamic court (in December 1993), he presented a written defense that we feel should be read from every pulpit. We carry a copy of it in our Bibles:

> "Jesus Christ is our Saviour and He is the Son of God. To know Him means to know eternal life. I, a useless sinner, have believed in His beloved person

and all His words and miracles recorded in the Gospel, and I have committed my life into His hands. Life for me is an opportunity to serve Him, and death is a better opportunity to be with Christ.

Therefore I am not only satisfied to be in prison for the honour of His holy Name, but am ready to give my life for the sake of Jesus my Lord and enter His kingdom sooner, the place where the elect of God enter everlasting life, but the wicked to eternal damnation.

May the shadow of God's kindness and His hand of blessing and healing be upon you and remain for ever. Amen.

With respect, your Christian prisoner, Mehdi Dibaj"

Here is a native Iranian Christian, who despite his excruciatingly painful circumstances, resolutely remained loyal to his Master and to the Spirit of truth. Not for a moment did he consider compromising his faith to save his skin, because to do so would nullify the truth he spoke so passionately in his letter of defense. This saint who had been unjustly imprisoned and cruelly tortured ended his defense plea with a prayer for his accusers, invoking God's kindness and blessings upon them. He had obviously spent the time in that small cubicle praying for his enemies as he knew Jesus did and still does. Because of his tenacious devotion to seek His Kingdom and righteousness, no root of bitterness sprang up from within him to defile his Christian testimony.

Shortly after his release in answer to the fervent prayers of many, he disappeared again. This time his mutilated body was found in a ditch. Soon after, Pastor Haik Mehr, the outspoken general secretary of the

Assemblies of God in Iran, was kidnapped as well and brutally executed without a public trial—a gruesome reminder that the enemy is not a toothless lion.

Persecution comes with the territory! It is hard to understand sometimes, but remember, the Apostle Peter was released from prison for a season while the Apostle James was put to death. The Apostle Paul was imprisoned repeatedly, and released, but was finally beheaded. It takes guts to appropriate the grace to be a dedicated Christian.

What a contrast between President Clinton's and Pastor Dibaj's stand for Christian moral standards.

The Rabbinical council of the fastest growing branch of Judaism in the U.S.A., the Association of Conservative Hebrews (despite that name, it is very liberal), has announced that because so many people in their congregations were living together before marriage, an official doctrinal change was needed so as not to lose them because of traditional Judaism's "old-fashioned stance" on what once passed as morality. The council stated that the committed unions of the couples within their synagogues needed to have their rabbi's blessing, because "many honest and moral people" have been branded and hurt by this "outdated doctrine" and have left the faith. Wow! "Already it has caused other religious organizations to rethink their stand," the newsman reported. "The next step," he went on to say, "is that they must consider the unions of committed homosexuals who have been begging to have the same blessing as married couples."

And Satan chuckled!

Steadfastness in the face of adversity is the Apostle Paul's prayer for all of God's people. He prayed that we may be **"strengthened with all power . . . for the**

attaining of all steadfastness and patience..." (Colossians 1:11)

Amidst the extravagant demonstrations of the Holy Spirit that are currently evident in such abundance, let us remember the purpose of the power and anointing of God's Holy Spirit: He is filling us with the joy of the Lord, which is our strength. We are being strengthened so we can be steadfast in the truth, patient, and a help to those who are wobbling. (See Romans 14:1 and Romans 15:1) Being patient means continuing to pray for them with a holy hope, not writing them out of the Kingdom.

Hugs,

Paul & Gretel

Heavenly Father, grant me the determination
to be steadfast and patient in Jesus,
and manifest these fruits of Your Spirit in me.
Anoint me with the joy of the Lord
by Your most precious Holy Spirit.
Holy Spirit of Truth,
break through any spirit of deception in me,
reach my heart and mind,
and grant me the grace to pray for my enemies,
even as Jesus did and still does!
Bless me with such a steadfast devotion
to seek Your Kingdom and Your Righteousness
that no root of bitterness can spring up
from within me to defile my Christian testimony.
Amen.

Chapter 18

LOVE IS KIND

Dearly Beloved,

> **"He has told you, O man, what is good;**
> **And what does the Lord require of you**
> **But to do justice, to love kindness,**
> **And to walk humbly with your God?"**
> (Micah 6:8)

The Lord has been pressing us to consider how many times the Holy Spirit urges God's people to be kind to one another. It is not enough, Jesus taught, to just pray for a hungry man and send him on his way, he needs to be fed as well. The one gesture is religious, the other is kind. The former fulfills the law, the latter demonstrates the heart of God. You can not be loving and not be kind!

Proverbs 19:22 instructs us that, **"What is desirable in a man is his kindness..."** and we are warned in Proverbs 3:3, **"Do not let kindness and truth leave you..."**

If God requires that His people be kind and exhibit kindness, it behooves us to pay attention to the meaning of these words chosen by the Holy Spirit, and to examine ourselves to see if our actions have given us the right to be called "kind." One of the best and quickest ways to determine this is to ask the people with whom we are related the closest if they would describe us as being "kind," because, according to the dictionary, one of the amazing definitions of the word "kind" is Christian!

Then, how are we, as Christians, to act towards our fellow men and women so that the world might recognize that we ARE Christians? Jesus said, **"By this all men will know that you are My disciples, if you have love for one another."** (John 13:35) And **"...love is kind..."** (1 Corinthians 13:4)

Love and kindness cannot be separated. We cannot really love someone and not be kind to them! One of the nine cherished fruits of the Holy Spirit (Galatians 5:22) in those who have yielded to Him is the capacity to be kind to everyone.

The word "kind" is defined as: 1. *affectionate (and) loving*; 2a. *of a sympathetic nature, disposed to be helpful and solicitous*; 2b. *of a forbearing nature, gentle*; and 3. *of a nature to give pleasure or relief—agreeable*. Some synonyms of kind are: *tender, compassionate, gracious, generous, merciful, considerate, courteous, forgiving, warm, understanding*, and *tactful*.

If your family has some loving doubts as to whether kind is really an apt word to describe you, do not DESPAIR, just ask the Holy Spirit to REPAIR your understanding of what it means to be kind.

There is something very beautiful about the kindnesses with which the Lord Jesus graced the ordinary people. There was nothing condescending or judgmental about His words or actions as He went about proclaiming the Kingdom of God by exhibiting, as naturally as breathing, the divine nature of His Father's kindness and loving care for His children.

Jesus was kind to the Samaritan woman at the well and to the immoral woman who interrupted the dinner party to thank and worship Him.

Jesus was kind to Zaccheus the despised tax collector and to the Gerasene demoniac, in both cases truly giving credence to Romans 2:4, **"...the kindness of God leads you to repentance."**

Jesus was kind to the bereaved widow of Nain by raising her son from the dead, and to the unbelieving father by healing his epileptic son.

Jesus was kind to the misunderstood Martha who chose the wrong time to be busy and to her sister, Mary, by allowing her to listen to Him teach (which no rabbi would have permitted).

Jesus was kind to the thief on the cross.

Jesus was even kind to Peter who denied Him, reminding us of the truth of what Job 6:14 records: **"For the despairing man there should be kindness from his friend; lest he forsake the fear of the Almighty."** Thank you, Lord Jesus, for kindly restoring the Apostle Peter for our sakes!

In turn, Peter advised: **"... in** (exercising) **godliness,** (develop) **brotherly kindness ..."** (2 Peter 1:7) He knew what Zechariah 7:9 meant: **"Thus has the Lord of hosts said, 'Dispense true justice, and practice kindness and compassion each to his brother ...'"** Peter practiced kindness and compassion to the lame beggar at the Beautiful Gate of the temple, who implored Peter for money, but instead was given healing through the name of Jesus. (The beggar asked Peter for alms, but Jesus gave him legs instead!)

Paul could write in Ephesians 4:32, **"... be kind to one another, tender-hearted, forgiving each other, just as God in Christ also has forgiven you"** because the Lord Jesus showed him forgiveness rather than condemnation.

"Sow with a view to righteousness, reap in accordance with kindness ..." (Hosea 10:12) is as true today as it was when it was written. The Holy Spirit is prepared to help you walk this truth out in your life and you can bet that your family will help, too, if you will let them!

"To sum up, let all be harmonious, sympathetic, brotherly, kindhearted, and humble in spirit; not returning evil for evil, or insult for insult, but giving a blessing instead; for you were called for the very purpose that you might inherit a blessing." (1 Peter 3:8–9)

Hugs,

Paul & Gretel

Holy Father,
repair my heart where I despair of being kind,
especially to those who have not been kind to me.
I want to be kind like Jesus,
but sometimes I just don't seem to have much
kindness left in me.
Yet I know that there is a limitless supply of kindness
available through me,
because Christ Jesus is in me, and He is Love,
and Love is Kind!
Lord Jesus,
manifest Your kindness through me, I pray!
Amen.

Chapter 19

VESSELS OF MERCY

Dearly Beloved,

"...I will appear in the cloud over the mercy seat."
(Leviticus 16:2b)

"Blessed are the merciful,
for they shall receive mercy."
(Matthew 5:7)

"For judgment will be merciless to one
who has shown no mercy;
mercy triumphs over judgment."
(James 2:13)

When the Lord gently placed the words "mercy" and "merciful" in our minds as a subject of this Letter of Faith, we doubted that it was the Lord because, as I carefully explained to Him, "We have just written about being kind, Lord, and people will think we are stuck in a rut and get bored reading our letters!" (We are so good at giving God "unknown information!")

He immediately brought back to our remembrance a story that we had heard about the aged Apostle John. At the end of John's life, he used to be carried into homes packed with eager believers straining to hear the pearls of wisdom and revelation this revered favorite of Jesus would impart to them. The silence was charged with excitement and then his voice, strengthened by his strong convictions and the power of the Holy Spirit, would boom out the exhortation, "Love one another as

Jesus loves you!" There would be a rustling and waiting, but nothing more would be forthcoming.

Finally one of the elders in his disappointment would blurt out, "But John, that is what you said last time you were here! We want to hear something new!"

With a gentle smile, the Apostle John would sweetly ask: "ARE you loving one another as Jesus has loved you?" And they would bow their heads in shame and shuffle their feet in embarrassment. "Then I must continue to exhort you to love one another until Jesus Christ releases me to teach you something else." No wonder he was known as the Apostle of Love!

Then we understood that we were not to be afraid of repeating what is on God's heart.

Many believers are struggling with bewilderment, frustration, and judgment when they see other Christians failing to behave in a Christ-like manner. They wonder: "Why are we Christians not of one mind? Why do we fight with one another? Why do we not act like Christ? Where are the honest and loving leaders?" etc. BUT, God would have us remember that only He has the right to judge the heart and motives of people, and that He does so from the seat of mercy. Our mission is reconciliation, "**. . . God, who reconciled us to Himself through Christ, . . . gave us the ministry of reconciliation, namely, that God was in Christ reconciling the world to Himself, not counting their trespasses against them, and having placed in us the word of reconciliation.**" (2 Corinthians 5:18–19)

We are hearing so much these days through prophetic types of all kinds that God is about to pour His judgment upon the Church (other than "our spiritually correct" group, of course!) and upon the Western industrial nations, that it is important to remember that God ministers His judgment from the throne of mercy for the purpose of redemption. **"The Lord ... is patient toward you, not wishing for any to perish but for all to come to repentance."** (2 Peter 3:9)

Jesus was not sent to earth to judge, nor to destroy it and its people, but to restore a fractured relationship that Satan had orchestrated through the introduction of sin. Not until Jesus comes again will He wear the mantle of judge.

When God instructed Moses to place the Law (the Ten Commandments engraved in stone) in the ark of the covenant, He also provided for a seat of mercy to be carved out of the purest gold to be placed over the ark, where, He promised, **"...there I will meet with you, and from above the mercy seat, from between the two cherubim which are upon the ark of the testimony, I will speak to you..."** (Exodus 25:17–22) He was proclaiming visually that mercy was higher than judgment which is based on the letter of the Law. The tutor (the Law—see Galatians 3:24–25) was not to be greater than the Master Teacher!

In no way was the Law to become a god! God, **"...the Father of mercies..."** (2 Corinthians 1:3), wants a people who will be His image-bearers by extending redeeming mercy to a lost and hurting world of people who have the sentence of death upon them because of their sins. But, He also wants us to offer mercy to our loved ones who hurt and disappoint us. Our dictionary says that the word mercy implies compassion that forbears punishing even when justice demands it, and that extends help even to the lowliest or most undeserving.

Because God is merciful as well as just, He sent His Son to receive the punishment of all of us who believe

Jesus is His Son. He has made us who once "**...were dead in** [our] **transgressions ... alive together with Him, having forgiven us all our transgressions, having cancelled out the certificate of debt consisting of decrees against us ... He has taken it out of the way, having nailed it to the cross.**" (Colossians 2:13–14) THAT is mercy!

That is the Good News that Jesus asks us to bring around the world and into our own homes. When we receive His kind of forgiveness, we can not help but want everyone to experience the same kind of mercy that we have experienced.

That is not saying that He approves of or condones the sins that we commit. The sentence against us was real and just and fitting: GUILTY! But, the word "mercy" means "a reprieve from a fate of considerable severity, without implication." Reconciled with God through His mercy, we can start our life anew with a clean slate.

There are people who have sinned against us, and God is asking us to extend the same kind of mercy to them as we have received from Him, through the power of the Holy Spirit who lives within us.

Whether it is a parent that hurt us,
a spouse that betrayed us,
a child that has disappointed us,
a friend that has let us down,
or an authority figure that has misguided or
misused us, or any other painful suffering,

God is inviting us to be merciful (forgiving, tender-hearted, understanding, charitable, considerate, generous, giving, compassionate, and kind) toward them, that we might bear His image and, incidentally, that we might be qualified to receive mercy from Him and from each other when WE need it.

Think carefully about the people who inhabit your life and have had a direct negative impact upon your actions, emotions, and thoughts. Are there some to whom you would have difficulty offering mercy? Then you need to let the Holy Spirit heal and release you into His mercy flow!

First, lay your judgment of them and their actions and your unmerciful dreams of revenge and punishment on the altar of forgiveness, and receive your reprieve from Jesus Christ. Then ask God to use you to flow His grace and mercy over them like living water and watch how each of your lives will blossom. **"Blessed are the merciful, for** [you] **shall receive mercy."** (Matthew 5:7)

"...show mercy, with cheerfulness." (Romans 12:8), and the **"Grace, mercy and peace will be with** [you], **from God the Father and from Jesus Christ, the Son of the Father, in truth and love."** (2 John 1:3)

Hugs,

Paul & Gretel

Dear Lord Jesus,
I confess that I need mercy, not justice in my life.
Grace me with Your mercy for others
so that I might become
a vessel of Your mercy and a minister of Your love.
Amen.

Chapter 20

CLEANSED TO CULTIVATE

Dearly Beloved,

"Thus says the Lord God, 'On the day that I cleanse you from all your iniquities, I will cause the cities to be inhabited, and the waste places will be rebuilt.

'And the desolate land will be cultivated instead of being a desolation in the sight of everyone who passed by. And they will say, "This desolate land has become like a garden of Eden; and the waste, desolate, and ruined cities are fortified and inhabited."

'Then the nations that are left round about you will know that I, the Lord, have rebuilt the ruined places and planted that which was desolate; I, the Lord, have spoken and will do it.' "

(Ezekiel 36:33–36)

Oh, how our hearts sing to think of that day when the Lord will cause the wastelands of ministry fields to become like the garden of Eden, and the desolate cities of our churches to be strengthened and dwelt in again with His people living in peace and harmony with their God and with each other!

God promises that the world will know that He is who He says He is when they see the fruitfulness of His Church restored. But the Lord pointed out to us that, like all things in His Kingdom, this all starts with our own personal cleansing, because we Christians are to be:

Cleansed to cultivate!

We are all called to be cultivators as our Father is, no matter what our giftings may be. That means an investment of our time, thought, and energy to inspire, arouse, stir up, and excite our fellow Christians to grow in the Lord and in their understanding of Him. The whole essence of the meaning of "cultivate" lies in the descriptive phrase: *foster the growth of* as in **"...let us consider how to stimulate one another to love and good deeds ... encouraging one another; and all the more, as you see the day drawing near."** (Hebrews 10:24 & 25b)

There are so many wonderful, God-breathed ways to exhort and encourage the desolate. Our Father wants to restore not only His people, but the land on which His people live. Love, hope, faith, holiness, steadfastness, consideration for others, and trust in the truth are the wonderful crops that can grow in the rich soil of our hearts once they have been cultivated by the clean hands of Jesus.

If, however, His farmer/servants, cultivate His fields with "dirty" hands, or tongue, or spirit, the plant or person becomes unclean or infected as well! Farmers are careful not to contaminate a field with a blight, fungus, or destructive insect. They will burn a field or turn it under rather than have all their fields or their neighbor's fields infected.

It is interesting that doctors are now warning us not to forget to wash our hands before and after we touch food, or other people, or our own faces to protect us from transmitting germs and viruses that carry deadly diseases. The discovery of powerful ("miracle") antibiotics has made us careless about basic hygiene. Doctors know how swiftly a disease can affect whole cities. For example, because the Christian Scientist

Schools don't believe in vaccinating their children, the whole St. Louis area had a severe outbreak of measles.

Because we know something about the power to heal and deliver that is released through Christ's blood, do we Christians tend to touch things we ought not to touch? Do we no longer have a Godly fear for the cleanliness of our spiritual lives? *"It's O.K. if I (or we) do this or that because God will forgive me if I just ask!"* Are we so sure of His grace that we presume upon it, and no longer examine ourselves to see if we are clean? Do we resist the loving but corrective ministry (cultivation) of our friends and leaders that would break up our fallow ground and weed out the error and sin in our lives?

Many churches do not offer communion regularly, nor do they require a confession or repentance. Therefore they are not experiencing the cleansing of Christ's blood in forgiveness, and the fruit of changed lives in their members or leaders who have sinned. Some Christians, often in the name of tolerance, have allowed strange and unclean ideas and practices to be embraced within their churches in order to appeal to unbelievers. Things such as Yoga, martial arts, and prayer meetings with Muslims and Buddhists (who some have been deceived into believing pray to the same God that we pray to) defile and pollute the sanctuaries of the one true God. As a result, our land is diseased, our families are ruined, the sheep are left desolate, and the fortifications of our churches are torn down by these well-intentioned apostasies. God is calling us to be His servants, His partners, His witnesses—His farmers—to cultivate the crop of His Kingdom promises, but we cannot come to Him to receive our assignments with hands that have been infected by the sins and religions of this world.

God wants to rebuild His Church, which to many of

the "nations" around us, seems like a wasteland. Our "fallow ground" needs to be broken up in order to bring forth a harvest of righteousness. Our cultivating liberates the shoots from the hardened soil of religious rules and traditions that are choking the growth by preventing the water of the Holy Spirit from reaching the roots.

We also need to submit to His cleansing, cultivating, and separating. His forgiveness will heal the disease of sin, just as those powerful antibiotics do in our bodies, when we allow ourselves to be continually cleansed by His Holy Spirit. Then we will see "**...the cities ... inhabited, and the waste places ... rebuilt.**"

Hugs,

Paul & Gretel

Holy Father, cleanse me and cultivate me
so that I can work productively in Your harvest fields
without polluting or defiling.
I desire to be cleansed and to stay clean.
Please release Your resurrection power in me
to establish Your divine order,
Your holy cleanliness,
and fruitfulness
in my life.
Amen.

Chapter 21

DON'T LOSE HEART

Dearly Beloved,

"I do not speak to condemn you;
for I have said before that you are in our hearts
to die together and to live together."
(2 Corinthians 7:3)

While re-reading the Apostle Paul's second letter to the Corinthians, we were struck afresh with the great love that he carried in his heart for this struggling church. Although they must have known that they deserved a reprimand for their insensitivity, for their selfishness, and for their shallowness, they were shocked to hear that their actions had so grieved their founder. They were filled with sorrow that he was not pleased with them.

We sensed that their letter to him in reply to 1 Corinthians must have been filled with defenses and excuses as to why they had thought and acted improperly, because they were telling him that other "so-called" apostles did not seem to object so strongly to what was going on in their midst, and they were puzzled.

The Corinthians had hastened to expel the gross sinner in response to Paul's first letter, but in a manner not so much to bring about reconciliation as to rid themselves of a cause of offense. To Paul's distress, they seemed to have missed the heart of God that he was trying to reveal to them.

Paul had every reason to be discouraged over the

condition of this church, and others over whom he had labored with the Lord to establish and nurture, yet woven in this letter of explanation, exhortation, and warning is the sure thread of his love and hope for them—his declaration of ultimate love.

The Apostle Paul's letter does not sound like the cry of a despairing man, however, but of one who has spent time with God and has been freshly reassured by Him that out of the "mess" would arise a church worthy to be part of the bride of His Son. Oh God, give us all that same reassurance, we pray!

Paul had learned to look at things as God looks at them—to see the church with spiritual vision, rather than through the eyes of the flesh. **"Therefore from now on we recognize no man according to the flesh . . ."** (2 Corinthians 5:16) **"Therefore, since we have this ministry, as we received mercy, we do not lose heart . . .** (for) **though our outer man is decaying, yet our inner man is being renewed day by day."** (2 Corinthians 4:1 & 16)

Paul was declaring that he chose to see the church growing in spirit, rather than dwell on its stumblings and fumblings. We all need to learn this lesson!

If we listen with our spirits, we can hear God crying out to us through these words of the Apostle Paul's today: *"Don't lose heart over the fragmented condition of the church! Though our outer man* (read 'appearance of the church') *is decaying, yet our inner man* (read 'the true believer within the church') *is being renewed day by day."*

Beloved, no matter what you see of God's dealings with His people, do not give up on the Church: it is the Body of Christ, God's chosen instrument to reveal His character to the world.

It is easy to look around us and see the churches that once hummed with expectancy, power, and truth who, like the Galatians, started in the Spirit and are ending up in the flesh. We weep that their leaders have been so blinded by the god of this world "**. . . that they might not see the light of the gospel of the glory of Christ, who is the image of God.**" (2 Corinthians 4:4)

Sometimes our spirits are burdened with the knowledge that so many of the new fellowships which we saw established by eager adherents to the full gospel of Jesus Christ have begun to decay. Where once we experienced the presence of the Lord, there is now just a vestige of the former glory. Many churches that were once moving in the Spirit and in Truth, have just faded away, and the wounded saints involved have disappeared into their living rooms and have closed their ears to any call to re-gather.

We have received many letters from saints lamenting the fact that they are bored with their church because it has become stagnant ("foul from lack of movement" according to Webster's Dictionary). They are distressed that their corporate outreach has all but ceased. Others are wearied because their gatherings are so frenetic that there is no place for "**. . . teaching, for reproof, for correction, for training in righteousness; that the man of God may be adequate, equipped for every good work.**" (2 Timothy 3:16–17)

Yet these kinds of things were apparent to Paul even in his day. His response was to intercede for those churches for he had seen them fashioned by transformed people seeking to worship God. He recognized that many people brought into the assemblies their own preconceived ideas of what a church should be, and his constant task was to exhort them to lay them all down.

The Apostle Paul was willing to train them and model for them **"the simplicity and purity of** [his] **devotion to Christ."** (2 Corinthians 11:3) He was loathe to have to remind them that he was qualified by the personal call of Jesus Christ Himself, but he was willing to humbly reveal his sins, his afflictions, his persecutions, his triumphs, and most of all, his tender heart toward them in order to win them to the ways of the Lord. **"For out of much affliction and anguish of heart I wrote to you with many tears; not that you should be made sorrowful, but that you might know the love that I have especially for you."** (2 Corinthians 2:4)

To the church in Corinth, and to us, Paul says, **"...we look not at the things which are seen, but at the things which are not seen; for the things which are seen are temporal, but the things which are not seen are eternal."** (2 Corinthians 4:18) There is more going on inside the hearts of believers than we can see with the naked eye! **"You are looking at things as they are outwardly"** Paul warns in 2 Corinthians 10:7. That is why we see decay and ruin, instead of growth and new life.

When a mature tree falls in the woods, it leaves an opening to the sunlight that brings increased growth for the younger trees that were under its protective umbrella. Do we weep for the loss, or rejoice over the new growth?

Surely we can only know how to respond righteously by seeking God's heart. We need to learn to weep when He weeps, and rejoice when He rejoices. There is something in our nature that makes it easier to weep over the loss of the old than to rejoice over the growth of the new! The Lord wants to adjust this in all of us.

We have a huge walnut tree down by the pond. Spring

came earlier this year and all the trees eagerly leafed out except this granddaddy walnut. Looking at its bare branches amongst all the verdant new growth surrounding it, we were tempted to think: *"It is dead. The grading on the new levee must have killed it."* But we know better! The walnut is always the last tree to come into full leaf, and it just wasn't its time yet. Now it has burst into full leaf and has put on a splendid stretch of new growth. How very sad it would have been if we had cut it down this spring thinking it was dead based upon what we saw on the outside!

Mercy keeps us slow to judge by what we see. Paul said: "**. . . as we received mercy we do not lose heart.**" (2 Corinthians 4:1b) God is presently doing something within each of us that is freeing us from the past and preparing us for the future. Even during these painful and perplexing times, hold fast to Him and to "**those who call on the Lord from a pure heart. But refuse foolish and ignorant speculations, knowing that they produce quarrels.**" (2 Timothy 2:22 & 23)

Please do not misunderstand what we are saying! There are churches that are dead, or dying, and the dear saints involved do not even know it yet. God is tearing down some churches and sifting through the rubble to rebuild the "waste cities" with cleansed stones to hold His glory for the world to see and marvel at.

Some churches are called for a particular season as well as for a specific reason. When God's reason for a church is over, to try to extend a divine season by fleshly activities and effort is not only futile, it is counterproductive. We need His discernment to know when we should pray for a "resurrection," or just attend the funeral!

Sadly, there are also highly "successful" churches

that exhibit all of the appearances of Holy Spirit manifestations on the outside, but are riddled with sin and strife and corruption on the inside. But, thank God there are churches today that are bursting with the new life of Jesus and are witnessing the power of the Holy Spirit flowing out from them into their communities. These are growing at an awesome rate, so rejoice, and don't lose heart.

"Therefore, having these promises, beloved, let us cleanse ourselves from all defilement of flesh and spirit, perfecting holiness in the fear of God." (2 Corinthians 7:1), and expectantly await His next move.

It is His move, and we believe that all of us are going to be thrilled to see the life that comes forth, even from some places that we had once judged were dead!

Hugs,

Paul & Gretel

Oh Lord, please give me the ability to see myself,
to see others, and to see the Church as You see us.
Gift me with eyes that see the renewing
that is going on inside,
not just the decay that is apparent on the outside!
Anoint my eyes, oh Lord, with Your eye-salve
so that I will be able to see the way You see,
and not lose heart.
Amen.

Chapter 22

FOR THIS WE ARE KEPT

Dearly Beloved,

"And about the ninth hour
Jesus cried with a loud voice, saying,
'Eli, Eli, lmana sabachthani.'"

(Matthew 27:46 as translated from the Aramaic or Eastern version of the Bible)

The last line is an Aramaic idiom that means:

"My God, My God, for this I was kept!
This was my destiny—I was born for this!"

All versions of the Gospels have retained these words in the original Aramaic tongue that the Galileans spoke at the time of our Lord—but given them a different meaning by the Greek and Latin translators: **"And about the ninth hour Jesus cried out with a loud voice, saying, 'Eli, Eli, lama sabachthani?' that is, 'My God, My God, why hast Thou forsaken Me?'"**

Nowhere in our western, popularly-accepted versions of the Bible is there recorded a more heart-rending cry than the agonizing question that Jesus is reported to have cried loudly from the cross. And yet, everything we have learned of the relationship between our heavenly Father and His beloved Son Jesus challenges this purported cry of bewilderment and despair that indicated Jesus could believe God had forsaken Him!

Did not Moses assure the Israelites in Deuteronomy 31:6, **"Be strong and courageous, do not be afraid or tremble at them, for the Lord your God is the one who goes with you. He will not fail you or forsake you."**?

And did not the writer of Hebrews describe God's faithfulness by declaring: "**. . . for He Himself has said, 'I will never desert you, nor will I ever forsake you,' so that we confidently say, 'The Lord is my helper, I will not be afraid. What shall man do to me?'** "? (Hebrews 13:5–6) The disciples and the women from Galilee never for a moment could have thought that Jesus said that God had forsaken Him.

As the anniversary of the Resurrection draws near each year, we are again confronted with this incomprehensible interpretation of our Lord's last words—words that seem to put a lie to all upon which we have based our faith! Many sermons and treatises have tried to explain this discrepancy by reasoning that *"After all, God cannot bear the sight of sin, and therefore, because Jesus became sin for us on the cross, God could not look upon Him until after His death and resurrection."* But we have never been comfortable with this warped concept, "**For He looks to the ends of the earth, and sees everything under the heavens.**" (Job 28:24) God is not surprised by nor is He squeamish about sin. He is bigger than sin.

Although God does hate sin, He continues to love us even when we sin, and He holds a holy hope for us that we will "**come to** [our] **senses and escape from the snare of the devil . . .**" (2 Timothy 2:26). We understand that we can forsake God during a trying time, or after having had a disagreement with Him, but we know that even, "**If we are faithless, He remains faithful; for He cannot deny Himself.**" (2 Timothy 2:13) Our hearts implore, *"Did You really forsake Jesus, Father? We can't believe that You and He were not One, to the very end, or that the Holy Spirit was not there too, comforting You! How can we reconcile our picture of*

You from the Scriptures and our own experience with You with the shocking repudiation we read in this translation of this verse?"

Have you noticed how God has a habit of answering your queries? We delight in prowling through secular, as well as Christian bookstores, eager to pounce upon a new find to which the Holy Spirit leads us. And so, when our eyes fell upon a particular book entitled: *Idioms in the Bible Explained and A Key to the Original Gospel* by George M. Lamsa in a back aisle of The Baptist Bookstore in Little Rock, Arkansas, our curiosity was piqued. This book was originally written by Lamsa in 1931 and republished in 1985. We knew that the Holy Spirit had lead us to this book.

George Lamsa was a world-renowned Bible translator and commentator. He was raised as a Christian in what was then an Assyrian community in the Middle East where the same Aramaic tongue used in the first century was still being spoken. Jesus spoke Aramaic, though like every Jewish man, He understood and read Hebrew.

Aramaic was the language spoken in the Fertile Crescent until the thirteenth century when it was mostly replaced by a sister tongue which we know as Arabic. Parts of that region have escaped modernization, and so the language, as well as the customs and idioms are miraculously preserved!

Lamsa contends that to answer some of the puzzling questions we have about the Scriptures we must study the age in which the Gospels were written, and explore the Eastern sources of the language and the beliefs of the early Eastern Church. The Assyrian Church which was founded in the early part of the first century A.D., was for many centuries the strongest branch of the Christian church in the world. At present it is still using the Aramaic language and maintaining the early apostolic customs in practice and worship. Despite the passage of time, the Assyrian people and land have remained much as in Biblical times.

Translating idioms is a problem in every language and culture. Idioms, colloquial expressions particular to a group of people, are almost never quite able to be translated literally into a comparable idea in another language. These phrases that are immediately understood within the culture that uses them, need to be laboriously explained to others.

For example, in America we use the expression, "I am in a pickle!" When someone tells us that, we quite properly feel empathy and offer to help because we understand that person is in trouble or a "tight spot" (oops, another idiom!) But how do you suppose a visitor from China, or almost any other country, would translate that statement? They might think literally, *"How can you get inside a brined cucumber?"*

The Greek and Latin translators of the Bible who were not familiar with the native idioms of the East, in many cases painstakingly let the Aramaic words in each Gospel stand as literal phrases. Later, this idiom was "translated" as a quotation from Psalm 22 because it starts similarly with **"My God, My God,"** and much of it does foretell Jesus' agony on the cross. So we in the Western world have just accepted the mistaken interpretation as an integral and therefore true part of the Bible. Of course Jesus and the New Testament writers used Aramaic idioms and metaphors without explanation because they were well understood by the hearers and readers of their day.

A good example is when the apostle Paul warned the Philippians **"Beware of the dogs..."** (Philippians 3:2), they all knew that he was saying, *"Beware of gossips and troublemakers!"* The first century Jews would know that the references about laying gifts at the Apostles' feet in Acts 4 & 5, did not literally mean placing their gifts in front of the Apostles like a gift to a potentate or a sacrifice to an idol. Instead, that descriptive phrase was used to mean that the gifts were given freely to be used at the Apostles' discretion.

Now, let us go back to the verse that opened our letter because it is paramount to understanding that God did not abandon Jesus, and therefore He will never forsake you. According to Mr. Lamsa, "Jesus did not quote the Psalms. [Psalm 22:1] If He had He would have said these words in Hebrew [the language of the Old Testament] instead of Aramaic, and if He had translated them from Hebrew He would have used the Aramaic word 'nashatani,' which means 'forsaken me,' instead of the word 'shabacktani,' which in this case means, 'kept me.'"

Today in Syria, this ancient Aramaic idiom is still spoken by those who suffer or are about to die unjustly: "My God, My God, for this I was kept ... this was my destiny—I was born for this." They do not complain of their lot, but trustingly embrace God's plan for them. Because of this attitude, Middle Eastern people rarely commit suicide!

When Jesus called out from the cross that time-honored Aramaic idiom: *"My God, My God, for this I was kept."* (or, *"I was born for this: This is my destiny."*), it was a cry of victory, not despair! It was a shout of triumph addressed to God, His Father, to celebrate with Him, declaring, *"It is finished; I've done it!"* He had successfully lived a sinless life and resisted every one of Satan's attempts to make Him take the easy way to Kingship.

This loud proclamation of victory was also a word of comfort to His followers and a reprimand to His detractors and torturers. No one had been able to thwart God's plan which Jesus had agreed to before He was sent to earth, and the timing of which was settled in the session of agonized prayer with the Father the night before in the Garden of Gethsemane. **"Now My soul has become troubled; and what shall I say, 'Father, save Me from this hour?' But *for this purpose I came to this hour.* Father, glorify Thy name."** (John 12:27–28a)

Jesus trusted His Father implicitly and humbly bowed His head in submission to Him that night in the garden, ready and willing to finish His task as a man here on this earth.

Jesus knew that He was to be the supreme and final sacrifice that would end the reign of sin and death over humanity. Christ's death on the cross and glorious Resurrection had been predicted in the Old Testament. He knew that His sacrifice would grant eternal life for those who believed and entered into God's invisible Kingdom now, and eternal damnation to those who refused to acknowledge the truth and continued to go their own way.

His Father promised to be with Him all the way and He kept that promise!

Whenever we commemorate Christ's death and Resurrection, let us recall the uplifting and victorious meaning of His last proclamation. It is a declaration of assurance for us who carry the torch of His truth, hope, and light. Now we can understand why we refer to that day as Good Friday!

We have Good News to share with the lost and lonely, the rejected and the disenfranchised, the hurting and the prisoners! That is why He chose us and granted us eternal life: "*...for this WE were kept!*"

Let's get on with it!

Hugs,

Paul & Gretel

Lord Jesus,
thank You for Your faithfulness to Your Father's plan.
Thank You for declaring fulfillment
instead of abandonment.
Help me to really know that You, our Father, and
the Holy Spirit, will never leave me,
abandon me, or forsake me!
And please, Lord Jesus,
empower me to be
forever faithful
to You.
Amen.

Chapter 23

THANKS—GIVING AND RECEIVING

Dearly Beloved,

"He who offers a sacrifice of thanksgiving honors Me;
And to him who orders his way aright
I shall show the salvation of God."
(Psalm 50:23)

"For even though they knew God,
they did not honor Him as God,
or give thanks;
but they became futile in their speculations,
and their foolish heart was darkened."
(Romans 1:21)

The Scriptural admonitions to give thanks to our God and praise His Name are multitudinous, and the benefits promised with our thanksgiving are mighty. The results of our not giving thanks are too monstrous to meditate.

It is a great privilege for us to be able to honor the Almighty God of the universe! And yet this awesome privilege is as simple as giving thanks to Him! Well, maybe not quite that simple because the Word says, "offer a SACRIFICE of thanksgiving."

The implication of these words is that it is costly to give thanks to the Lord. But look at the gain: we honor Him; we will see the salvation of our God, and we will please the Lord more than with the sacrifice of any physical possession. The body builder says, "No pain, no gain!" But what is their gain compared to ours as thanks givers?

As we searched the Scriptures to review "thanks" and "thanksgiving" verses, we were amazed to find how very few there are in the Gospels compared to the Epistles, and compared to the great number in the Old Testament Law and Prophets. We were even more intrigued to realize that with only two exceptions, the "thanksgiving" Scriptures in the Gospels were all recording Jesus giving thanks to His Father as He broke bread and initiated Communion.

The first of these exceptions is Luke 2:36–38, "**And there was a prophetess, Anna ... And she never left the temple, serving night and day with fastings and prayers. And at that very moment** (the moment Joseph and Mary brought the newborn baby Jesus to the Temple) **she came up and began giving thanks to God, and continued to speak of Him to all those who were looking for the redemption of Jerusalem.**"

Anna recognized Jesus as the Messiah, and gave thanks to God! She literally restarted the flow of thanksgiving to God from His people that had apparently dried up for well over 400 years. That's right, chronologically the last time the word "thank," or "thanks," or "thanksgiving" is used in the Old Testament is in Daniel 6:10 where Daniel "**...continued kneeling on his knees three times a day, praying and giving thanks before his God, as he had been doing previously**" even though he knew that King Darius had decreed that anyone caught praying to another "god" beside himself would be thrown into the lions' den.

Daniel gave the ultimate sacrifice of thanksgiving: he put his life on the line! And God fulfilled Psalm 50:23 in his life by closing the lions' mouths, and using that to bring King Darius to see the light of God's salvation: "**I make a decree that in all the dominion of my kingdom**

men are to fear and tremble before the God of Daniel; for He is the living God and enduring forever, and His kingdom is one which will not be destroyed, and His dominion will be forever. He delivers and rescues and performs signs and wonders in heaven and on earth, Who has also delivered Daniel from the power of the lions." (Daniel 6:26–27)

The only other reference to giving thanks to God in the Gospels, except where Jesus gave thanks to His Father, is in Luke 17:11–18. Jesus cleansed ten lepers, and then (verse 15), "**. . . one of them, when he saw that he had been healed, turned back, glorifying God with a loud voice, and he fell on his face at His feet, giving thanks to Him. And he was a Samaritan. And Jesus answered and said, 'Were there not ten cleansed? But the nine—where are they? Were none found who turned back to give glory to God, except this foreigner?'** "

Obviously it was rare to hear thanksgiving to God in Israel, even after a healing miracle had been received!

Jesus modeled how to give thanksgiving to the Father to the people of Israel. When He fed the multitudes, initiated the Lord's Supper, and prayed, He publicly gave thanks.

The Apostle Paul constantly emphasized the giving of thanks to God IN all things and FOR all things: "**in everything give thanks; for this is God's will for you in Christ Jesus.**" (1 Thessalonians 5:18) and, "**always giving thanks for all things in the name of our Lord Jesus Christ to God, even the Father;**" (Ephesians 5:20) He exhorted the young Church to give thanks to God so repeatedly because they apparently were not in the habit of doing so! "**And let the peace of Christ rule in your hearts, to which indeed you were called in one**

body; and be thankful." And, **"Devote yourselves to prayer, keeping alert in it with an attitude of thanks-giving."** (Colossians 3:15 & 4:2) Paul was concerned lest they fall back into the state of thanklessness that he addressed in Romans 1:21, and consequently their foolish hearts became darkened.

Every November, Americans celebrate the national holiday of Thanksgiving. It honors God to give Him thanks for the mighty things He has done, and for the mighty things yet to come from His hand, and it is God's will for all of His people.

We should remind each other to thank God for the answers to those hasty little personal "flash prayers" that He has graciously granted. Remember the answers to the simple requests that no one else even knows about, the sweet secrets just between you and Him—the ones you haven't even "formally" prayed for. These answers show you that He is aware of your unspoken thoughts even about everyday things. Express to Him your awe and delight over His intimate care for you!

I remember such an incident a few years back that is etched on my heart. We had a long drive down a gravel road to our mailbox. Once there, we had to turn around and drive back and that took some careful maneuvering to avoid getting stuck in the ditches on each side of the road. "If only the county would widen the opening of our road and lay some gravel on it, we could simply turn around," I sighed as I tugged on the steering wheel of our 20-year-old farm truck.

A week later, as I approached the mailbox, I had to rub my eyes in disbelief—there was fresh gravel spread on a widened entry to our road, just as I had imagined! I burst into thanksgiving! We still suspect that it was done by angels, because our poor county just doesn't normally do that kind of maintenance.

God saw the desire in my heart and provided it! Because of my great prayers of faith? No! Because of His great love for me! Selah! (that means pause and think about that).

Let us all learn to pour forth our thanksgiving so that Jesus will never say of our land, **"Were none found who turned back to give glory to God?"**

Let's all make thanks a major part of our daily walk with Jesus!

Now is the time to establish this bench mark in our walk with God: "**...in everything...**" and "**...for all things...**" being thankful and making thank offerings. If we learn now to give thanks for the abundance that often means so little, then in the future we surely will abundantly give thanks for the little that will mean so much.

It seems to us that America is becoming a thankless nation. Less and less do we hear a heart-felt "thank you," which along with "please" is one of the "two magic words" of our youth that seem to be vanishing from the American vocabulary. It is disturbing to us to see this trend affecting the Christian community.

Thankfulness in the heart must be expressed outwardly through word and deed. But thanksgiving must also be graciously received! Some of our brothers and sisters in Christ seem to have also lost the ability to receive thanks!

Example No. 1: We said to a worship leader after a service: "Thank you! That was beautiful! We were really blessed!" She quickly responded: "It is all Jesus! Don't thank me! Praise the Lord! Give all the glory to God."

Two hurtful things happened in this exchange. First, our thanks was brushed off so we felt disappointed, frustrated, and put down because our thanks was not received. We knew her voice was a gift from God, but we wanted her to know how much her use of it blessed us! Second, she was deprived of the encouraging appreciation that God has prescribed for all of us for good spiritual and mental health.

Example No. 2: We said to a friend as we were parting: "God be with you!" He responded offhandedly: "He is!" instead of saying "Thank you—I appreciate that blessing!" His flip answer quenched the Spirit and we were both robbed of the blessing of thanksgiving.

The primary reason for these experiences is a lack of understanding of God's grace and how we are to respond to it. God has created us to need loving affirmation from other people as well as counsel and correction. These are usually provided by the Holy Spirit flowing through members of the Body of Christ. If we cannot learn to accept positive inputs, we surely will struggle with receiving corrections! Even worse, we may subconsciously seek gratification of our God-given need for affirmation from some unlawful (spiritually speaking) source.

Please understand that you are not usurping God's glory by receiving compliments and thanks for something splendid that God has done through you! You only do that when you respond with thoughts of conceit and pride.

Learn to graciously receive compliments, praise, and thanks. Enjoy them without embarrassment! Then, at the end of the day, present each one as a thanksgiving offering to your Heavenly Father. *"Thank you, Father, that Paul and Gretel liked the song You gave me, and took the time to thank me. That blessed me, Father,*

and really made me feel good. Now I take that praise and give it to You as a thank offering."

One of our sweet friends sees affirming compliments for how she is used by God as a lovely bouquet of flowers gathered throughout the day to present to Him in the evening before going to sleep. Thus God actually gets double glory; once when He uses your gifts and talents, and again when you give Him back the blessing you received from the person who He ministered to through you.

A godly way to receive compliments and thanks and blessings is by saying: "Thank you! That is a real blessing to hear, and I accept it gratefully." You are accepting the thank offering of the person you have been used by God to bless, and you are firmly receiving the praise as a trophy to present to your God. The circuit of grace is thus completed to the full glory of God.

Join us in learning together to give God thanks continuously for all things and in all times along with the angels and saints around the throne of God, proclaiming **"...blessing and glory and wisdom and thanksgiving and honor and power and might, be to our God forever and ever. Amen."** (Revelation 7:12) May thanksgiving always be found in your heart and on your lips, and may you learn how to give and to receive thanks and praise to the glory of God the Father.

Hugs,

Paul & Gretel

Heavenly Father, I can hardly start to pray without bursting into thanks for all You are in my life, and for the unfathomable riches of Your grace to me and to my family. Even now, I thank You for showing me that You bless thanksgiving, and that when I am thanking You, I am joining all of the hosts in heaven around Your throne in honoring You, and your Son! I recognize that sometimes I have been ungracious in responding to praise. Help me to receive compliments and blessings in a way that honors You. Release through me a spirit of continual thanksgiving so that wherever I go and whatever I do, every life I touch will be filled with thanks to You. Amen.

Chapter 24

FROM SCHOLARSHIP INTO FELLOWSHIP

Dearly Beloved,

"Not every one who says to Me, Lord, Lord,' will enter the kingdom of heaven; but he who does the will of My Father who is in heaven. Many will say to Me on that day, 'Lord, Lord, did we not prophesy in Your name, and in Your name cast out demons, and in Your name perform many works of power?' And then I will declare to them, 'I never knew you; depart from Me, you who practice lawlessness.'"
(Matthew 7:21–23)

These are frightening words from our Lord Jesus! I dare say that all of us have on occasion shuddered deep inside as we have read these words, and thought: "Dear Lord Jesus, let me know You and Your will that I might never be lawless in Your sight! That I might never hear You say to me 'I never knew you!'" Yet we all can get so involved in DOING FOR Him that we overlook opportunities to establish and cultivate and develop our personal relationship with Him—a close intimate companionship where we both get to know each other!

Our dear friends Lou and Lil Carey, who minister to men with addiction problems at Dunklin Memorial Camp in Florida, recently wrote to us: "No disciple ever wants to hear the words, 'I never knew you.' To be certain those words are never spoken to us, we must really get to know Him!" And then he pointed out that if we do not make the effort to really know Jesus, He won't get to know us!

That is what really penetrated our hearts and stunned us as we read their letter. Of course we all understand that He "knows" us—after all the Scripture says he knew us before the beginning of time and while we were being formed in our mother's womb. But we are talking about deep, intimate, "down-to-earth" knowing—a two-way street of communication, emotion, and understanding. As Lou said, "If we don't abide with Jesus throughout the day, He observes our impulsive reactions, our most personal characteristics, and our behavior in difficult circumstances—but He doesn't live them WITH us. He is left on the outside, as a patron watching a performance, but He is not a participant!"

So we are confronted with the challenging concept that He cannot really get to know us until we make the decision and take the action to really know Him, not just know about Him, even if we know a whole lot about Him! Observe that Jesus' admonishment in Matthew was not: "Depart from Me, for you never knew Me!" But rather He said: **"I never knew you!"**

We can only know Him as we dwell in His word and live our lives in and with Him. Jesus said in John 8:31–32: **"If you abide in My word, then you are truly disciples of Mine; and you shall know the truth, and the truth shall make you free."** And in John 15:4 (Amp.) Jesus promised: **"Dwell in Me and I will dwell in you—Live in Me and I will live in you . . . "** Dwelling—living—abiding—is an inside relationship that is deeper than intellect or emotion, but includes both! This is the only way we can we continue growing in our knowing of Him—and then He will know us!—because, intimate "knowing" is a two-way street!

Lou challenged us by saying: "An example of leaving Jesus on the outside would be to ask ourselves, 'How would Jesus respond in this situation?' We thus consider Jesus, but in a performance mode, not a servant-disciple mode, and we then operate on our own understanding of the character of Jesus."

Have you ever asked yourself that question in a hard spot? We have! But that is not turning to the indwelling Jesus! It is turning to our knowledge about Him, instead of our life with Him!

Lou poignantly points out that rather we should ask: "Jesus, how would You have me respond in this situation?" This is the way we walk in the reality of abiding in Him, and of His abiding in and with us. This is how we learn to know Him, and He gets to know us!

As He so often does when He brings us new revelation or adjusts us in former ones, Jesus brought a second witness to us in confirmation of this truth from Lou's letter. The witness came in the delightful person of our daughter, Alexis, as she related a powerful experience she had with Jesus during a conference she had just attended. The speaker was emphasizing the need for us all to draw closer and have a more real fellowship-relationship with Jesus. He had asked the question: "If you could enjoy a whole evening sharing one-on-one with anyone who has ever lived, who would you choose?" He hesitated, and then he said, "I suppose that most of you are thinking—Jesus!" He smiled and let that set in.

During this time, Alexis was taken into the Spirit realm, and she experienced herself sharing with Jesus around a cozy fire in her living room. She was reveling in the anointing of His presence and the love for each other that was flowing heart-to-heart, when the speaker continued: "And of course these are the things you would be discussing with Jesus: 'What did You write in the sand at the feet of the pharisaical men who brought the woman caught in adultery to You for judgment? What did You say to the disciples as they walked with You on the road to Emmaus on the day of Your resurrection? What did Elijah and Moses say to You that glorious time on the Mount?' "

Alexis almost exploded out loud: "No! No! No! You don't understand! I am not sharing questions about Him that the Holy Spirit can (and does) answer for me as I meditate with Him in God's Word! I am reminiscing with Him about the times we shared victories together and gave each other 'high fives' as we came out into the light again after a long, dark walk through the valley of the shadow of death together; I am reliving His deep, healing, comforting love as He ministered to me through the disastrous times we shared; I am giving and receiving love as I have never before experienced from any other human being; I am reveling in His presence and marveling at His enjoying mine!"

Which of these two saints is holding Jesus "out-there somewhere" and which is abiding with Him, inside, in reality?

Beloved, we are being led to discover a reality in our walk with Jesus as never before. We are being confronted with a major choice to move:

From SCHOLARSHIP into FELLOWSHIP

God wants us to realize that our very lives, yes even our salvation, depends on our choosing FELLOWSHIP as well as SCHOLARSHIP—our choosing to know Him, as well as to learn about Him—and our choosing to be real with Him as well as to be doctrinally correct.

Of course we need to learn as much as we can about

Him from reading the precious truths in the Scriptures! But that is not enough by itself, especially if the learning is kept merely intellectual, and not appropriated into our spirit and emotions, and then practiced in our daily walk with Him. If we choose wrongly now, we risk hearing Him say to us on our final day:

"Depart from Me, I never knew you."

Beloved, if this intimacy with your living and loving Lord Jesus is unfathomable to you right now, don't despair! Ask the Holy Spirit to lead you to Him in a new level of intimacy. Ask Him to heal the wounds and rejections and judgments you have suffered that are preventing you from fully entering into His life and allowing Him total access to the inner person of your heart.

Seek prayer ministry from someone who does walk in this precious fellowship with Him, so they can help you be healed of your wounds and cut free from the sins that so easily entangle you and that build a wall of separation between you and your God. **"Do not give sleep to your eyes, nor slumber to your eyelids; deliver yourself like a gazelle from the hunter's hand, and like a bird from the hand of the fowler."** (Proverbs 6:4–5) until the Lord of Hosts set you free!

Beloved, it is our prayer that this letter will stir something in the very depths of you so that you will call out to your God for reality and intimacy in your walk in the Spirit with your Lord, Jesus! No matter how good or how close your walk with Him is today, Beloved, there is MORE!

We strongly sense in the Spirit, that in order for us to stand as overcomers in the whirlwind that is poised over the whole world, parts of which are already being torn asunder by its force, we are going to need this kind of inside, real, and personal bonding with Jesus just to survive with a testimony for His glory.

Hugs,

Paul & Gretel

Precious Lord Jesus,
when I hear someone pray who really knows You
like a dear and trusted friend as well as Lord,
I long for that kind of intimate relationship with You.
Please remove from me anything
that is holding me back from abandoning myself
to a living and abiding fellowship with You.
Please, Lord, draw me so close to You
that I will know that You know me.
Amen.

Chapter 25

CLEAN OUT THE LEAVEN

Dearly Beloved,

"Clean out the old leaven . . ."
(1 Corinthians 5:7)

It's springtime! It is time to throw open the windows and shake out the winter blankets. It is time to send the rugs to the cleaners and wash the winter grime from the windows.

Yes, Beloved, it's time to roll up our sleeves and clean our spiritual house and let the fresh air in! When a dear friend shared with us that the Lord was directing her to pray "FRESHNESS" for us in the upcoming year, our hearts leapt with anticipation. We sensed that the stale winter of our spiritual life was coming to an end, and began to yearn for a vibrant new breath of the Spirit to tear down the cobwebs of spiritual dullness that had insidiously begun to drape over us.

Traditionally the Jews would virtually dismantle their homes once a year, hauling all the past years accumulation of refuse and foodstuffs out to the pit. They were ruthless in their search for uncleanness of any type so that their homes would be pure enough to receive the Messiah on the celebration of the Passover. The leaven with which they baked their bread was carried out, and the house was leavenless until the new fresh leaven was allowed to be brought in. After the scrubbing and cleansing, it then was time to light all the lights and display the purity of their home!

We are reminded of King Hezekiah's command to his

priests and their response as recorded in 2 Chronicles 29:5 & 16 "**'Listen to me, O Levites. Consecrate yourselves now, and consecrate the house of the Lord, the God of your fathers, and carry the uncleanness out from the holy place.' ... So the priests went in to the inner part of the house of the Lord to cleanse it, and every unclean thing which they found in the temple of the Lord they brought out to the court of the house of the Lord.**"

Would you believe that God frowns on sweeping dirt under the rug? Matthew 10:26 says, "**...for there is nothing covered that will not be revealed, and hidden that will not be known.**" The things that we don't want to deal with now can't just lie undetected under a beautiful carpet of rhetoric or good deeds; sooner or later they will begin to smell.

We are convinced that our neglected sins have a tendency to multiply as well. One neglected sin is like a runaway amoeba—kept in the dark, it multiplies and, much to our horror begins to hump up the rug with its progeny. People begin to notice that we keep the shades down and the lights low in hopes that no one will spy the beast under the rug. He who wants us to be beckoning "lights of hope" in a dark and frightening world is not pleased to see His temple shrouded and unclean.

We sense the Holy Spirit is urging us all to give our spiritual temples a thorough spring housecleaning! What He has asked us is, *"Are you willing to spend some uninterrupted time evaluating your life, cleaning out the musty old ideas, attitudes, and mind-sets, and washing down the very walls and foundations of your heart? Will you ask Me for the courage to disencumber yourselves of sins and useless clutter, even those you find hard to part with?"*

"Of course," we said, "yes Lord!" But we found that it takes a discerning eye, a firm resolve, and steady perseverance to be a clean and wholesome temple for His indwelling.

All of us need to take a good look at some of the possessions that we value so highly—for instance, those large leather-bound account books on our desk. We have spent hours painstakingly recording every trespass perpetrated against us so that we can share them with Jesus, but they are of no value to us, and the fact is, He would be offended to see them, because **"love . . . does not take into account a wrong suffered. . ."** (1 Corinthians 13:5d) They have to be hauled out to the incinerator! The house cannot be clean enough for the Holy Spirit to dwell in while those books lie there emitting foul clouds of defiling judgmentalism.

Throw open your cupboards and take stock of your reserves. Have you been feeding your family stale manna? Hoarded up manna will grow worms! Beware of the laziness that would prevent you from gathering fresh manna daily. Some of those treasured teachings you gleaned from those old audio tapes or sermons that tickled your ears should be taken out and reexamined in the light of your increased knowledge of the Scriptures and of the ways of the Lord. Stop serving and eating baby food, and start preparing meals for yourself and family using solid meat and fresh vegetables.

Be willing to eat bread without your favorite leaven for a while. The leaven might be a well-known and well-worn commentary; a church doctrine that predigests God's written word to fit its traditional stance on a subject; a book of devotions, or even a prized "family recipe" on how to "rightly divide the Word." Prepare to receive and welcome new leaven when it arrives, and you will never miss the old.

Stock up on some fresh new teachings and experiences of the Holy Spirit. Instead of dining on other people's adventures (like stale leftovers or frozen TV dinners), start exploring the recipe book (the Bible) again, to bake mouth-watering and nourishing meals. Sure it takes time, but the effort is worth it for the taste and for the peace of knowing what the ingredients are.

There are some gifts that He gave you long ago that are lying neglected beneath musty old traditions and mind-sets such as dispensationalism ("The time for the manifestation of healing and the verbal and power gifts of the Holy Spirit has passed"), Nicolaitanism ("niko" = to conquer or suppress; "laites" = the people: i.e. "only leaders are endowed to use the gifts"), or male chauvinism ("Only men are allowed to minister in the congregation").

We need to take our precious divine charismata off the shelf, dust them off, read the directions again, and begin to use them to heal, deliver, encourage, and bless others. Begin to use them first in your home with your family, then with your guests, then with your congregation, and finally out in the world.

Open the doors and sweep out the dirt that has been carried into your temple on the unclean feet of others. When filthiness is brought in by a friend or by a member of the family, we often tend to let it lie there rather than offend the carrier. This would be a good time to repent of that and insist on getting it out! A slurring remark; a nasty jab; a crude jest; critical gossip; a lewd joke; a careless but hurtful gesture: whatever unclean spirit was let loose in God's temple must be thrown out.

Sometimes guests have carried bitter or contentious

spirits in with them that pollute the atmosphere. A television broadcast might have sprayed forth violence or lust. Don't let it settle on your clean walls and rugs! Immediately demand that the unclean spirit leave and disinfect your home with praises to the pure Heavenly Father! With expressions of encouraging love to one another, and washings with the Word of God, His peace will return and reside!

Take down some of those old pictures from the wall. You know the ones I mean: the portrait of Jesus as an emaciated Italian fop as painted by a court artist, the portrayal of God as a gruff old man with a long white beard seated on the throne of judgment, and the depictions of angels as curvaceous, blond women with long hair and enormous wings, or as fat, pink babies. How can we hope to recognize God in our lives if those ungodly images are still hanging on the walls of our mind?

Go ahead, move the furniture; it will give you a new perspective on life. If you have been sitting in the same spot for years, your view certainly isn't as exciting as it used to be. For instance, if you have been reading the lamenting Psalms every day for the past umpteen years, try dwelling in a new chapter of Proverbs each day in the month, or read Colossians aloud to yourself every morning. Return to the Gospels and observe the walk of Jesus from the new vantage point of your increased spiritual maturity and knowledge of Him.

Ask the Holy Spirit to show you new ways to pray from your new view out the window. Perhaps you'll need to tear up your prayer list and ask God to confirm to you what names HE wishes to have you continue to pray for and which names He wants you to drop, or to add. He may shift you from praying about individual needs to interceding for nations or ministries. Instead of pleading for the salvation of your unsaved family and friends, you may find yourself being led to pray for a special anointing for the workers that God has chosen to harvest them for the Kingdom. One of our dear friends was lead to change from praying for his unsaved loved ones, to praying for his unloved saved ones!

New vistas and changes in your prayer life will encourage your faith and give you new hope. These changes may seem drastic at first, but we all need a fresh outlook. It's healthy! Be a trend-setter in your spiritual neighborhood!

If your windows are dulled with the grime of winter, wash them with the living waters of the Word of God to improve the clarity of your outlook and vision. Your home will sparkle with a fresh new light of God's presence. Remember, others should be able to see in and observe the character of Jesus in your home life. Anything that obscures that witness has to submit to a purifying scrubbing—and God's kids DO "do windows!"

The front window of our old farmhouse is festooned with crystal prisms of all sizes and shapes that shoot forth dancing rainbows when the sun catches them. We keep them sparkling by frequent bathing in soap suds for we have found that they quickly lost their ability to release the dazzling displays when dust was allowed to accumulate on their many faceted surfaces. When we have just washed them in a bath of suds, they explode the sunshine into dancing rainbows all around our cozy blue-and-white living room. But as the dust collects on them day by day, they start to just display muted streaks. Nothing brings life back to its full brilliance like a good scouring!

Prepare your home for the coming of the Lord. It is a temptation to just snuggle down into our unmade beds and slumber away another productive season, but we implore you to leap up and strip that bed of procrastination. Beat the lethargy out of the mattress, and turn it over. Wash the sheets and blankets and hang them out on the clothesline in the sun and brisk air. Open the windows wide and invite the fresh breeze of the Holy Spirit to fill your home, blowing out the mustiness of a stagnant winter.

"For this reason you be ready too; for the Son of Man is coming at an hour when you do not think He will." (Matthew 24:44)

Hugs,

Paul & Gretel

Lord Jesus, I want to be ready for You!
Whether You come tomorrow,
or a millennium from now,
I want to be clean and fresh and
prepared for Your return!
And I want to be a comfortable place
for Your indwelling right now!
Please clean my house with me Lord
so that abiding in me will be pleasing to You and
the Holy Spirit of our Father.
Amen.

Chapter 26

DO NOT FEAR

Dearly Beloved,

"And there will be signs in sun and moon and stars,
and upon the earth dismay among nations,
in perplexity at the roaring of the sea and the waves,
men fainting from fear and the expectation
of the things which are coming upon the world,
for the powers of heaven will be shaken . . .
But when these things begin to take place,
straighten up and lift up your heads,
because your redemption is drawing near."
(Luke 21:25–26 & 28)

FEAR: "*1. A feeling of anxiety and agitation caused by the presence or nearness of danger, evil, pain, etc.; timidity, dread, terror, fright, apprehension. 2. Respectful dread, awe, reverence. Example: Fear or reverence of God.*" (Webster's New World Dictionary)

The first definition of fear describes an insidious and infectious disease that tries to entrap us and paralyze our expectation, faith, and motivation. It nibbles and gnaws on the weakest links of our thoughts and rushes in like a flood at the heels of bad news, disturbing circumstances, or alarming lies. Fear attacks our faith unless we are equipped to recognize it and prepared to resist its advances.

Remember the fable about Chicken Little? An acorn making its way to the ground glanced off her noggin (that's American slang for "head") and without taking time to discover the truth, off she raced, full of fear and assumption, to be sure that the king received the dire news that the sky was falling. On her way she proclaimed to anyone who would listen that the world was coming to an end, striking fear in their hearts as well.

There certainly is plenty of frightening news to be heard today—some true, some conjecture—from the lips of friends as well as the ever-present media news "presenters." But Beloved, we must examine the message carefully with divine discernment before we spring into action. For example, although the specter of the devastation from an "impending Global Warming" has now been proven by the vast majority of respected geophysicists to be just another journalistic hype encouraged by some inexperienced scientists in order to be able to qualify for large government study grants, it is almost impossible to dispute the error or calm the public. We can remember the scare and hoopla just 30 years ago about a new Ice Age that was supposed to be forming quickly—sigh! Memories and honesty are seemingly both still in short supply!

The important thing that we Christians must remember is that the Lord Jesus Himself exhorted us to keep our heads and not to faint with fear but to **"straighten up and lift up our heads because our redemption is drawing near."** He can be trusted with our lives. In the midst of the earthquakes, the hurricanes, the floods, and the fires, He promises to be with us—not necessarily to save us from suffering, but to strengthen and love us through the catastrophe. He who is our redemption makes Himself known to us as our **"present help in time of trouble"** whatever that trouble may be:

"God is our refuge and strength,
a very present help in trouble.

Therefore we will not fear,
though the earth should change,
And though the mountains slip
into the heart of the sea;
Though its waters roar and foam,
though the mountains quake at its swelling pride."
(Psalm 46:1–3)

A dear friend of many years shared a remarkable story with us. Nancy, a widow, married a widower, and started a new and exciting life at the age of 60, which included learning to fly her new husband's company plane so that she could land it in an emergency. One spring they were returning from a trip to California, cruising high in the clouds on autopilot, when she noticed the artificial horizon (an instrument that shows the flying attitude of the airplane) at a 45 degree slant earthward! Neither of them had felt anything strange immersed as they were in the clouds, but they knew their high-tech instruments were warning them of trouble.

Their autopilot had jammed "nose down!" Her husband quickly began to try to rectify the terrifying problem. It took all of his strength to wrestle for control of the plane—trying desperately to over-ride the autopilot—and at the same time, instruct Nancy how to disengage the power from the malfunctioning equipment. They were diving well over the red-line (maximum safe) airspeed before she could get the fuse out of the autopilot circuit. The gravity forces in his pull-out popped the landing gear out and caused other structural damage to the wing, but they cleared the ground and were able to fly to the nearest airport for an emergency landing.

To her relief and surprise she felt no fear during these traumatic moments! "I knew that death was not the end. I was sustained by faith which flooded me with a calming peace. I felt sad for my daughter who would not have her mother at her upcoming wedding, but I knew that the Lord could and would handle that problem as well. I know now that I will never fear for my life again, for I have faced death and know that it has no hold over me."

That, Beloved, is faith tried in the furnace!

Jesus said:

"Peace I leave with you; My peace I give to you; not as the world gives, do I give to you. Let not your heart be troubled, nor let it be fearful."
(John 14:27)

Our prayer partners Dick and Caroline are also sterling examples of unfailing faith under pressure. They are both suffering indescribably nerve-racking pain that cannot be relieved medically. These brave spiritual war horses were miraculously healed by the Lord of these conditions years ago when He recruited them and asked them to sign on with His army (Dick is a retired three-star Air Force General, a WWII hero, and former head of NATO). They have tirelessly and effectively served God from one end of the world to the other: humbly getting up at 4 a.m. to make breakfast for the student body at YWAM Camp; sleeping on mats on the floor of huts in Indonesia for weeks while bringing the message of God's good news to the natives; praying for the lame, deaf, and blind and seeing God heal them in front of their eyes; escaping from Armenia in the middle of the night as the revolution and earthquake exploded all around them—to name just a few of their adventures in the service of the Lord.

Now, in their seventies, the blinding pain has returned, but they continue to worship the Lord and to walk in faith, and to teach all who have ears to hear about God's divine plan and love. Neither death, nor a life of pain, has power over them. "Nothing is going to separate us from the love of God or the faith we have in God's faithfulness" they assure us—and we stand in awe!

Jesus said: **"These things I have spoken to you, that in Me you may have peace. In the world you have tribulation, but take courage; I have overcome the world."** (John 16:33) The prince of the power of the air, Satan, has always tried to use fear to enslave us, to render us too frightened to function or too fearful to flee or fight his fabrications. He endeavors to persuade us that God doesn't really care about us. But Jesus Himself said: **"...the very hairs of your head are all numbered. Therefore do not fear; you are of more value than many sparrows."** (Matthew 10:30–31)

The Apostle Paul writing to the Romans reminded us Christians: **"...you have not received a spirit of slavery leading to fear again, but you have received a spirit of adoption as sons by which we cry out, 'Abba! Father!'"** (Romans 8:15)

As Christians, we do not have to fear punishment from our Father. His discipline is forgiving, loving, corrective, and redemptive. The fear of the Lord that we read about in the Scriptures does not mean a frightened cowering, but to be overcome with reverence and respect for His holiness and power. We cannot help but fall to our knees in His presence, for **"...we have come to know and have believed the love which God has for us.**

God is love, and the one who abides in love abides in God, and God abides in him ... There is no fear in love; but perfect love casts out fear, because fear involves punishment, and the one who fears is not perfected [matured yet] **in love."** (1 John 4:16 & 18)

The Lord Jesus predicted that there would be **"wars and rumors of wars"** (Matthew 24:6), yet we are not to panic but to seek Him for wise counsel and continue to **"believe the love which God has for us."** Disease "monsters," seemingly immune to medical weapons, lurk in the shadows threatening to pounce upon the unsuspecting. AIDS, hepatitis, chronic fatigue syndrome, Lyme disease, staph infection, and that old nemesis, T.B., have some Christians shaking in their boots. Others are afraid to eat or drink certain things because of news that it might be harmful. Their lives are being dictated by their fears, not by their faith.

As you watch the days ahead unfold, set your mind to rejoice that GOD IS NOT NERVOUS—no one or no thing is going to thwart His plan!

Despite Millenniums of severe financial, political, religious, and medical upheavals in the world, the human race has survived, because God isn't finished with us yet.

Do you know that there were a third more people living in the world at the beginning of the 14th century than there were at the beginning of the 15th century? The Hundred Years' War; the two waves of Black Plague starting in India and sweeping all the way to Iceland; persecution and slaughtering of thousands of Jews; financial disasters; earthquakes, volcanoes erupting; plus another crusade or two, polished off people from one end of the earth to the other. The church and the governments were corrupt, and lawlessness ruled the earth. BUT GOD continued to call His people out of the darkness into His glorious light, and the good news about Jesus Christ has survived to bless us and all mankind with ears to hear.

Join us in shouting that we believe our God is more powerful than all the evil forces of the whole world put together! Face fear and fight against it with faith in Father God.

Hugs,

Paul & Gretel

Lord Jesus,
grace me with the courage of the Lion of Judah!
Help me to keep my mind set
on the things of the Spirit,
and not on the things of this world that are so scary!
Help me to encourage my brothers and sisters
to know that You are our God,
and that all authority in heaven and earth
has been given to You,
and that You are always with us,
and will never forsake us, even to the end of the age.
Grace me, Lord, to fear not amidst all of the fearful,
and to despair not amongst all of the despairing.
Release in me faith to overcome fear and declare:
". . . as for me, I trust in Thee, O Lord, I say,
'Thou art my God.' My times are in Thy hand;
deliver me from the hand of my enemies,
and from those who persecute me."
(Psalm 31:14–15)
Amen.

Chapter 27

ABOUNDING LOVE

Dearly Beloved,

"And this I pray, that your love may abound yet more and more and extend to its fullest development in knowledge and all keen insight—that is, that your love may [display itself in] greater depth of acquaintance and more comprehensive discernment; so that you may surely learn to sense what is vital, and approve and prize what is excellent and of real value—recognizing the highest and the best, and distinguishing the moral differences; and that you may be untainted and pure and unerring and blameless, that—with hearts sincere and certain and unsullied—you may [approach] the day of Christ, not stumbling nor causing others to stumble."

(Philippians 1:9–10 Amp.)

The word "love" has become so hackneyed (made trite and commonplace by overuse) in the last century that it is hard to apply it appropriately these days. Only those who have been privileged to experience love as an all-encompassing, ever-growing, constantly endearing, and always delightfully new bonding can try to explain the joy of living in love.

True love is a love that continues to grow in joy; it is a love that overshadows the weaknesses and transgressions that occasionally are revealed in the beloved one; it is a love which tenderly forgives, and quickly forgets.

To be a recipient of this kind of unqualified love humbles us and inspires us to love as we are loved.

We receive this kind of love from our Father God, and pray to receive it from our spouse, family, and closest friends. It is, however, the love that humans can express only by the active grace of God working in their lives!

The Apostle John explains it so beautifully for us in 1 John 4:19: "**We love, because He first loved us.**" We have the ability to love as He loves us because He loved us enough to die for us so that we can live—and love—through Him.

Listen to the definition of love listed under "theological" in the dictionary: "a. God's benevolent—kindly—concern for mankind, and b. Man's devout attachment to God!"

Notice that the Apostle Paul does not just pray that we might have better discernment! He prays that our love would increase and deepen until it influences every thought and subsequent word and action!

He knew that if we received godly knowledge, insight, and discernment into a truly loving heart, we would not be drawn into heated arguments, or the breaking of relationships over different practices or various viewpoints that have little to do with the tenets of Christianity that Jesus and His apostles taught with their words and their lives.

Our respect and affection for our brothers and sisters in the faith should enable us to listen to them kindly, discuss our differences with them freely and lovingly and honestly, continue in fellowship with them, and humbly learn from one another. Inviting others to approach the throne of grace and wisdom together with us, in love and prayer, tears down the walls of separation and judgment.

The Apostle Paul's prayer is that our "devout attachment to God" will increase so that we would absorb all that God is revealing to us through the knowledge of His Spirit and His word, and crowd out all that is superfluous or irrelevant to our position with the Lord in His Kingdom. As we come to know and love Jesus at a deeper relational level, our discernment will become more acute, so we can sense what is vital to His heart.

We shall then, by His grace, be enabled **"to make a distinction between the holy and the profane, and between the unclean and the clean"** (Leviticus 10:10), **"...to discern between good and evil"** (1 Kings 3:9 and Hebrews 5:14), and to **"...extract the precious from the worthless."** (Jeremiah 15:19)

As we are trained by the Holy Spirit to recognize **"the highest and the best,"** we shall be able to **"approve and prize what is excellent,"** and ignore the tawdry temptations to be drawn after unclean physical or emotional desires, the persuasions of man's ideas, traditions, or positions, or the beguiling attacks of the enemy.

Learning to **"distinguish the moral differences"** between what is being offered to us in increasingly appealing packages on television, in movies, and in music recordings, and that which is written for our instruction in the Scriptures about the pure and righteous behavior of Jesus, protects us from becoming tainted, dirty, defiled, blamable, and guilty.

We practice keeping our hearts in tune with His heart through His grace, mercy, and forgiveness, and by listening carefully to the loving words of correction from our Christian family and friends.

All of us yearn to have **"hearts that are sincere and certain and unsullied"** so that we would have no cause to dread the day of Christ's coming. None of us can bear the thought that we might stumble, or cause someone else to stumble, because we lack knowledge of God's ways and His "benevolent concern for mankind."

The good news is that we do not have to live in fear, "white-knuckling" our way along the highway of holiness, biting our fingernails in anxiety, stressing ourselves into a frazzle trying to perform to an unachievable standard of behavior. God is more interested in the motivation of our hearts than in the correctness of our doctrine, and His grace is sufficient for us!

Through the cross of Jesus, God offers us the way into His Kingdom and His perfecting. When we nail our self-will and indulgent desires to His cross, we declare that we recognize our sin and enable Him to transform our lives. We then enter into His rest, and yield to Him as His grace works in us to know and to do His will.

In His famous Sermon on the Mount as recorded in Matthew 5:6, Jesus promised us: **"Blessed are those who hunger and thirst for righteousness, for they shall be satisfied."** If we refuse to sit at anyone else's spiritual or moral table but our Lord Jesus Christ's, we will always have a place set for us, we will always know His love, we will always feed on righteousness, and we will always love with His kind of love.

Beloved, we pray: **"May you abound in and be filled with the fruits of righteousness (of right standing with God and right doing) which come through Jesus Christ, the Anointed One, to the honor and praise of God—that His glory may be both manifested and recognized."** (Philippians 1:11 Amp.)

Hugs,

Paul & Gretel

Lord Jesus,
help me in my frustration with learning true love.
I see Your model of perfect love,
and I am humbled and in awe of it.
I confess my love for You and
for special people in my life,
but I know how far short of Your love I fall
even with them.
But Lord Jesus, You are love, and You dwell in me!
Please love through me until I can get it right,
which I guess will be for ever and ever.
But that's OK with me because
at least I'll get in on it,
and because I know that when You come,
I will be like You in all things,
even in the totality
of Your love.
Amen.

Chapter 28

WITHERED CORN AND EMPTY PONDS

Dearly Beloved,

"For I will pour out water on the thirsty land
and streams on the dry ground;
I will pour out My Spirit on your offspring,
and My blessing on your descendants . . ."
(Isaiah 44:3)

The Lord has quickened in our hearts words that He spoke to us during the last period of severe dryness in our area: *The withered corn and empty ponds reveal the state of much of My Church today!*

We can all learn something about ourselves, about God, and about our relationship with Him from the continuing droughts in parts of our country and the world.

The Bible frequently illustrates the renewing of God's revival with the refreshing of rain. The above verse from Isaiah is just one such example.

The saints who are living in drought, like the American Midwest experienced in the early 1990s, are very much aware of the lack of rain and are praying according to 2 Chronicles 7:13–16 for a soaking from the heavens (both physically and spiritually). But it is hard to motivate saints in areas of the world that are not experiencing a drought to pray for rain—it would interfere with their plans and projects.

Similarly, those in the Body of Christ that are recognizing spiritual dryness are praying for the outpouring from heaven, but those that think things are going very nicely are not. The trouble is that the whole Body of Christ, the Church, desperately needs a fresh anointing from God, whether it knows it or not!

God has established a principle in the Bible of revealing the spiritual in the natural: as surely as nature needs timely moisture to give birth, and to grow, and to mature, the Church needs the rain of God's Spirit!

Let us share what we see God showing us about the Church and ourselves as we observe the effects of the physical drought we have experienced here at Eagle's Nest Farm. We do not share in condemnation, but rather in the spirit of calling us all to be alert during these hot and dry times that can so often lull us into a kind of spiritual weariness and exhaustion. Remember, it is in the dry times that a cool drink of water is a most appreciated gift, and it carries its own special reward. (See Matthew 10:42 and 25:31–40) **"Like cold water to a weary soul, so is good news from a distant land."** (Proverbs 25:25)

Withered Corn: The new life (ear of corn) that is forming in the field is being stunted in its growth by the lack of moisture. In the worst cases, the tassels required for pollination are not forming at all, so no kernels will even appear on the stunted ears. In the dry church, the "newborn" in the faith, are similarly restrained from maturing; and in the worst cases, the outreach is so impotent that there are no new believers even being grown for the harvest.

In some fields there are places that have received or retained more moisture that others, so there are some promising looking ears of corn. But corn, like a person in the church, needs strong neighbors to survive and grow into full maturity. In fact, in spiritually dry times we need each other more than ever to keep from withering because we form shade for each other's roots of faith. Even in "healthy" times, we (like the cornstalk) need each other for support to stand against strong winds of adversity.

As the corn plant is progressively starved for water and scorched by the sun, the leaves curl up so that they are no longer open to the sun's rays. The process of photosynthesis is increasingly reduced, until the plant can derive no benefit at all from the sun—just receiving the withering heat, but not the life-giving energy. This is an accurate picture of some of the Spirit-starved saints who have shut themselves up and turned inward, and are no longer able to draw strength and growth from the Son of God.

Beloved, we ought not ever let that happen to us! We must constantly remind ourselves that because we believe in Jesus, we have rivers of living water coming forth from our innermost being! We need to learn to drink deeply from these rivers within ourselves and from within our brothers and sisters, and to release these rivers in us for others to drink from.

Empty Ponds: The continuing drought has kept the water level of the ponds falling steadily so that successive levels of fish spawning beds have been exposed to the withering heat of the sun, dried out completely, and overgrown with weeds. This means that the fish have not been able to bring forth new life even though they are repeatedly laying eggs.

This represents many churches that are progressively getting so dry and devoid of the Holy Spirit's manifest presence that they cannot bring forth any new believers. **"We were pregnant, we writhed in labor, we gave birth, as it were, only to wind. We could not**

accomplish deliverance for the earth nor were inhabitants of the world born." (Isaiah 26:18)

This situation in the natural also speaks to some church environments where there is a little anointing of the Holy Spirit, but it is quenched before any real new life can come forth. Then the leadership may permit some release of the Spirit, but it is withdrawn before it can be fulfilled in changed lives. The sheep, like the fish in our ponds, keep trying to multiply because that is built into their nature by their Creator, but there needs to be a steady or rising level of Holy Spirit anointing to bring forth Holy Spirit multiplication!

There is still enough water in the ponds to sustain the life that is already there, and to water others like the thirsty deer that appear ghost-like out of the woods, but it is warm and has lost its refreshing and quenching quality. Revelation 3:16 indicates Jesus' attitude toward the lukewarm: **"So because you are lukewarm, and neither hot nor cold, I will spit you out of My mouth."** The pond life is getting increasingly sluggish, and even unresponsive to our feedings. The longer the drought continues, the more chance that the water itself will become de-oxygenated or contaminated—and fish will die!

As the pond level recedes and stays low for extended periods, tree saplings, weeds, and brush spring up on the embankments. They send their thirsting roots deep down into the soil to seek the moisture of the water it has absorbed. If they are allowed to remain, they will weaken the levee and eventually cause it to leak when the water level returns to normal. Therefore, it is very important to keep the levee clean of undesirable growth while the water level is low. It is amazing how well the worthless weeds and nasty nettles grow during weather too dry for more fruitful things to grow. However, we found that the low water level is also a good time to clean up the debris that has collected along the shore below the "normal" waterline.

Correspondingly, it is most important that we saints keep ourselves pure and "weeded" during spiritual dry times, so that when God pours Himself out upon us again, we will not leak the blessings and be ruined. This is a time of yielding to His cleansing and purifying so that we will be trustworthy vessels when God pours out His Spirit in might and power!

The need to keep alert to entrapments in the dry times was demonstrated for us during one of our early morning prayer walks in the woods. We seemed to be getting cobwebs in our faces much more often than usual (a most uncomfortable feeling). Then we realized why. There was no dew! It had been so dry that we were not even getting our shoes wet as we walked in the tall grass. On a more normal morning, our shoes and socks would be soaked from the dew when we got home. There were no sparkling diamond specks of dew highlighting the webs so that we could see them before we walked into them. Like the dew, the anointing of the Holy Spirit allows you to discern, avoid, and tear down entrapments that would otherwise ensnare you.

We noticed also that many of the trees had leaves gnawed away by insects as well as browned by the drought. Rain cleanses as well as feeds! In dry times we need to be especially vigilant to keep away the devourer in all his insidious forms.

What will happen now when it does rain?

When we get a little sprinkle, the curled leaves immediately open and lift up, as though to praise God, but only the very shallow roots get watered. The weeds seem to benefit tremendously, because their roots are shallow, but the trees and the deeper-rooting and more valuable bushes, shrubs, and vines (the fruit-bearing vegetation) seem to get very little help. It does not take long before their leaves are all curled up again after a brief shower.

A soaking downpour, however, reaches the deep roots so that resurrection life begins to flow again. The devouring bugs are washed off the leaves and the fruit seems to start swelling to maturity even as we watch. The pond levels rise with fresh, cool water that drowns out the brush and weed growth on the banks, and even though it looks muddy at first, it is fresh and cool and rejuvenating.

Beloved, we all need the rains of refreshing—the soaking downpours of the Holy Spirit! God has promised it to us if we will yield to Him personally, and on behalf of the Church, and for our nations!

"And it shall come about, if you listen obediently to my commandments which I am commanding you today, to love the Lord your God and to serve Him with all your heart and all your soul, that 'I will give the rain for your land in its season, the early and late rain, that you may gather in your grain and your new wine and your oil.'" (Deuteronomy 11:13–14)

"Repent therefore and return, that your sins may be wiped away, in order that times of refreshing [the rains of the Spirit!] **may come from the presence of the Lord; and that He may send Jesus, the Christ appointed for you . . ."** (Acts 3:19–20)

This particular verse in Acts clearly says to us: no revival, no Return! We also think the world is presently facing the serious situation of: no revival, no survival!

God gave us the assuring answer to the physical and the spiritual drought: praise, repent, and pray! "**Then Solomon stood before the altar of the Lord in the presence of all the assembly of Israel and spread out his hands toward heaven. And he said, 'O Lord, the God of Israel, there is no God like Thee in heaven above or on earth beneath, who art keeping covenant and showing lovingkindness to Thy servants who walk before Thee with all their heart . . .**

When the heavens are shut up and there is no rain, because they have sinned against Thee, and they pray toward this place and confess Thy name and turn from their sin when Thou dost afflict them, then hear Thou in heaven and forgive the sin of Thy servants and of Thy people Israel, indeed, teach them the good way in which they should walk. And send rain on Thy land, which Thou hast given Thy people for an inheritance.'" (1 Kings 8:22–23 and 35–36)

Our prayer is that God's mercy will triumph over judgment in all our individual and corporate lives. So, Beloved, at times of dryness especially, be sure to sow mercy that you might reap mercy! Then when rain does come, we can stand with upturned faces and rejoice with all of nature and heaven.

May the renewing, refreshing, and life-giving anointings of the Holy Spirit rain fresh and abundantly upon you.

Hugs,

Paul & Gretel

Heavenly Father,
I feel so dry at times that
I wonder if I can continue to bring forth the new life
You are calling forth from me.
My prayer times seem withered, and
I am constantly ensnared by cobwebs in my thinking.
I need an outpouring of Your blessed Holy Spirit!
Please pour Your Spirit on me, in Jesus' Name.
And keep pouring and keep refreshing me
so I will always be fruitful for You.
Amen.

Chapter 29

POWER NOT TO STUMBLE

Dearly Beloved,

"...His divine power has granted to us everything pertaining to life and godliness, through the true knowledge of Him who called us by His own glory and excellence. For by these He has granted to us His precious and magnificent promises, in order that by them you might become partakers of the divine nature, having escaped the corruption that is in the world by lust.

Now for this very reason also, applying all diligence, in your
faith supply
moral excellence, and in your moral excellence,
knowledge; and in your knowledge,
self-control, and in your self-control,
perseverance, and in your perseverance,
godliness; and in your godliness,
brotherly kindness,
and in your brotherly kindness,
Christian love.

...for as long as you practice these things, you will never stumble; for in this way the entrance into the eternal kingdom of our Lord and Savior Jesus Christ will be abundantly supplied to you."

(2 Peter 1:3–7 & 10b–11)

The Apostle Peter, the Lord's irrepressible exhorter and Kingdom ambassador par excellence, never tired of reminding believers of the joys of developing into the image of Christ through obedience to His word and example. His epistles are an impassioned plea to believers not to forget what Jesus has done for us on the cross and who He is today in our lives. He could not bear to think that his beloved friend and Lord's death would be for naught in our life through our being careless with the truth, forgetting His promises, stumbling into unbelief, and returning to our former way of life, and therefore, eternal separation from God!

So concerned was Peter for our lives to be a reflection of Christ's character (so that we would be useful and fruitful in the knowledge of our Lord Jesus Christ—see verse 8) that he did not hesitate to warn believers over and over of the dangers that could occur from ignoring or disobeying the Lord's commandments.

Peter knew that unless these nine graces that the Lord had taught him were increasing daily in our lives by being strengthened through commitment and disciplined practice, we would become vulnerable again to the siren calls of our flesh, the world, and the devil. He reiterates his concern and determination in the next few verses: "**...I shall always be ready to remind you of these things, even though you already know them, and have been established in the truth which** (Who?) **is present with you. And I consider it right, as long as I am in this earthly dwelling, to stir you up by way of reminder ... And I will also be diligent that at any time after my departure you may be able to call these things to mind.**" (2 Peter 1:12–13 & 15)

It behooves us to spend some time focusing on these verses and asking for divine understanding of what the Holy Spirit was saying through this compassionate Apostle. With this realization flooding our minds, we can better make a concerted and daily effort to cooperate with Him to increase in these essential traits of Christian character, not only to keep ourselves from stumbling, but to exhibit the consistent character of Jesus to others. Then we will be demonstrating the truth of the gospel of Jesus Christ through our sanctified behavior. This is the greatest witnessing tool we can use.

Let's examine the meanings of each of these nine progressive virtues.

- **Diligence:** *A steady, earnest, and energetic application and painstaking effort*
- **Faith:** "*. . . that leaning of the entire human personality on God in absolute trust and confidence in His power, wisdom, and goodness . . .*" (Hebrews 10:22 Amp.)
- **Moral:** *Just, good, honorable, decent, responsible, principled*
  Excellence: *Virtue, quality, worth, value*
- **Knowledge:** *Understanding, clear perception, something learned and kept in the mind*
- **Self-control:** *Restraint exercised over one's own impulses, emotions, or desires*
- **Perseverance:** *To persist in spite of difficulties, counter-influences, opposition, or discouragement*
- **Godliness:** *Purity, reverence, righteousness, God-fearing attitude*
- **Brotherly:** *As a close loyal kinsman or friend*
  Kindness: *Of a sympathetic, forbearing, and pleasant nature*
- **Christian Love:** *Deep self-sacrificing devotion; a passion to express and demonstrate one's ardor and respect for one another by words and actions that give glory to God in their unfailing purity*

The Apostle Peter exhorts us to apply a steady, earnest, and energetic effort in building our faith in who the Lord Jesus Christ is. The word "apply" means *to devote or dedicate yourself, work at, study, and concentrate on something.* It takes a concerted effort to guard our faith from the onslaughts of the enemy, our flesh, and the world's disapproval of our actions.

In our faith, we are to supply ourselves with moral excellence—that is, principled virtue. To the detriment of our witness, we Christians have sometimes trumpeted the importance of faith (as if it were an act of our will!) without submitting our impulsive words and actions to the gentle but firm hand of the restraint of moral excellence. Often the Holy Spirit will cause a verse to flow through our mind to show us the way. Sometimes a name or a face will pop into our consciousness and we remember what happened in another's life as they went this way. Other times, we might feel an uncomfortable, or sinking feeling, or something like "angel wings fluttering" in our stomach area. These are all gentle signals orchestrated by the Holy Spirit to make us stop, check, and consider the virtue of our plans.

The only way that we can learn moral excellence is by supplying ourselves with untainted knowledge and, at the same time, resisting the temptation to raise our collection of knowledge to an idolatrous position. That's where self-control must come in!

Interestingly, one of the meanings for the word "self" is "automatic" as in the words "self-starter" and "self-winding." Hmmm! By diligent practice of our faith, tempered by the virtues we learn through knowledge, we should eventually attain to a maturity in our lives where control of self becomes automatic! In other words, we make an advance decision to delay gratification as long as it is necessary to achieve the results we most desire, and we do not let our impulses supersede our ultimate desire, which is to obey and please the Lord.

It takes perseverance to hold on to that kind of decision. We must persist in spite of difficulties, counter-influences, opposition, or discouragement to obtain the prize. Consistency is the key to perseverance, because "practice ***does*** make perfect" or "practice brings automatic reflexes"—eventually. Self-control ***will*** become easier the more we persevere in exercising it. Self-will becomes weaker and less of a problem as it becomes atrophied from lack of use.

From the steady resolve and the practice of these virtues emerges godliness which brings such an unexpected explosion of grace. One does not just receive godliness as a gift at rebirth, (though we would like to have it happen that way—without effort), but by a track record of humbling ourselves to His will and accepting the suffering that that kind of determination brings into our lives: accepting it without complaint, knowing the joy that awaits us beyond the cross (Hebrews 12:2). To be identified with God and His Son, our Savior, because of who we are and how we deport ourselves, also brings delight here and now.

Because of this virtue living in us, we are then able to extend to others a brotherly kindness that is unselfish, pure, and without hidden motives. Our warm-heartedness and pleasant nature, characterized by mercy, will exhibit a love of even the unlovable. As we become willing to be inconvenienced for one another, there will arise in the hearts of those to whom we minister a trust and faith again in the goodness of Father God!

As we practice brotherly kindness, we will find ourselves being drawn up out of ourselves and our fleshly efforts and into the encompassing presence of

His love: a love that is so pure and clean and honest that it brings us to our knees in gratefulness, awe, and adoration of Him whose ways are so different from ours. We will long to present and extend that kind of pure love to all the hurting people around us that they might be healed and delivered and encouraged to press on into the center of that love too!

All the painstaking hours and days and years of training ourselves by His enabling power to ascend the steps into His love will suddenly be considered a small price to pay. Our friends and relatives will be blessed as they see us transformed into warm, unflappable, considerate human beings who are a pleasure to be around; people who listen carefully and offer real answers; people who are not trying to control other people's lives, but instead, are willing to gently and respectfully introduce them to the One who will lead them into the paths of righteousness—the One who will never leave nor forsake them.

Isn't this what Christianity is all about?

Right now, both of us are once again being led to apply diligence to some neglected facets of our faith to reinvigorate it and to transform us more into the image of Jesus. Won't you join us?!

Hugs,

Paul & Gretel

Forgive me, Father, for becoming careless
and taking for granted Your magnificent promises
that I might become a partaker of Your divine nature.
By Your grace,
I will start to apply diligence in my faith again
and make a concerted effort to supply that faith
with moral excellence
through a spiritual knowledge of
Your person and ways.
Help me to apply self-control to my life so that
I might persevere in my quest for godliness.
Please make my heart tender toward my fellow man
so that I will extend unqualified kindness and
Christian love to them
in the name of Your precious Son, Jesus.
Amen!

Chapter 30

DON'T MUZZLE THE OX

Dearly Beloved,

"Where no oxen are, the manger is clean,
But much increase comes by the strength of the ox."
(Proverbs 14:4)

I got to chuckling about this verse as I was washing our kitchen windows just after we returned from a nine week ministry trip to England. No matter how hard I try to keep the glass clean, the birds manage to splatter them right through the screen because we have bird feeders attached to the window frames. We enjoy watching the many goldfinches, woodpeckers, cardinals, and the rest of the birds "chow-down" at our various feeders and bathe in our all-weather birdbath. It brings us much pleasure (much increase of enjoyment)!

However, as I stood almost ankle-deep in thistle and sunflower seed husks, scrubbing the bird-poop off the outside of our windows, I seriously began to weigh the messings versus the blessings! What did I want more: to have a clean and picture-perfect lawn and sparkling windows, or to be able to enjoy the proximity of some of God's most colorful creatures while we eat in our cozy kitchen bay window? What gives more eternal value and pleasure?

Just then, a pair of downy woodpeckers swooped by impatiently, wanting me to leave their "picnic grounds," and the Lord brought the above verse from Proverbs to my mind. I shook my head at the silly comparison, but the Holy Spirit persisted. As long as we don't allow oxen to live in our nicely-scrubbed barn, we think we can safely show it off to our neighbors! But wisdom and experience tell us that much increase (*profit, gain, or revenue*) comes by having an ox to help with the work.

If we are going to allow an ox into our life, however, we are also going to have to expect to be cleaning up their mess in our barn! And you can safely bet that somebody is going to notice, and someone will complain, and others will talk unkindly about us! So the question is: is it worth all the trouble?

When our four children were all age seven and under, one of our dear friends and neighbors—who had one perfect son—ran over just before dinner to borrow a card table. I met him at the door with baby Philip in my arms and the other three children milling around me: one of whom had just filled his pants, and another was pulling on my skirt to ask for the fourteenth time when we were going to eat. As our neighbor hurriedly grabbed the table and left, he assured me that he loved coming over to our house because it made him appreciate his own quiet home so much more! In my unregenerated mind I considered hurling the fully-loaded diaper at his retreating back, but I was too busy retrieving the three year old who was trying to climb up the bookshelf after the cat!

People who live in a fantasy-world of faultlessness live in fear of something or someone "upsetting their apple-cart"—that is, their carefully orchestrated life, work, or ministry.

"What if someone in my family, business, or church makes a mess? What will people think of ME because they goofed?" is their constant cry. "What if I myself make a mistake? Maybe it is better that I don't do anything new or bold than risk doing something wrong." Many are afraid to take the risk to see if in the long run and in God's plan the "increase" is worth the disarray.

There are some churches who have fallen into that pattern. They only allow the pastor or priest or an "accredited" elder to teach, or to serve communion, or to counsel, or to prophesy, or to minister—or a "professional" musician to lead the worship. They keep tight control over every activity so that it will be a "perfect offering" to the Lord (or is it the visitor they are trying to impress?). They think they have a lovely, orderly, clean showplace, but in reality it is nothing but an empty, dull barn filled with religious "dentist's office" music! Those God-sent oxen (helpers) who bring their strengths and challenges into our well-ordered bailiwicks sometimes leave a heap to be cleaned up and a smell that has to be dealt with, but fields are plowed, seeds are planted and fertilized, and harvests are reaped!

The Great Shepherd knows that some of those gangling youths that seem to be all legs and stumbling feet (speaking chronologically or spiritually) will improve with patient instruction, loving modeling, and encouraging practice until they become seasoned servant/shepherds. But it takes time to train, nurture, and mature budding "profitable adults"—just ask any parent.

Don't fire them, train them! Don't squash them, exercise and encourage them! So problems do occur! Life is like that—problems are just part of living. God is not surprised by their existence. He wants us to consider them opportunities to learn new ways to walk with Him. We need to learn to face and deal with what arises unexpectedly, handle the problem righteously, and then move on.

We all learn through and from our mistakes! God assured us a long time ago that He would clean up our messes if we were willing to take the risk of learning to speak and move by His Spirit.

Jesus didn't give up on His disciples! His closest disciples contended for seats of honor (read "power") and, to His astonishment, even wanted to use their newly acquired gifts to call down fire on the Samaritans for rejecting their request for a night's lodging! He patiently but firmly corrected their attitudes and their impulsive bravado.

When Jesus came down from the Mount of Transfiguration, He found that the remaining disciples had "freaked out" over an epileptic child's seizure and He had to step in to kindly heal the young boy and to comfort the father who by this time had lost almost all belief. But He didn't take the reins away from His disciples because they had failed. He wanted them to learn by observing and then by doing, and then by trying again. He allowed them to make mistakes, and graced them with the ability to learn from their mistakes as well as from their victories. Can any of us do anything less?

The Apostle Paul followed in Jesus' footsteps. His epistles illustrate his willingness to encourage the early Christians to continue flowing in the gifts while he gently but firmly corrected them, and sometimes even rebuked them, for their impulsive actions. In no way did Jesus, or any of the Church's founding leaders, suggest that no one should minister until they "got it right every time," or had graduated from the "school of prophets," or had been approved by the accrediting board of the Sanhedrin!

Let us all determine to help, not hinder, each other

as we corporately travel this exciting road of spiritual maturing with our Lord Jesus!

Hugs,

Paul & Gretel

Lord Jesus,
I pray that You will help me to be tolerant and
patient with my brothers and sisters
as we try to learn to imitate You.
Teach me to learn how to encourage,
and not to criticize!
Direct my eyes to the increases,
and not to the messes.
Give me ears to hear those who would correct me,
strengthen me, and mature me
so that You can better use me
in bringing forth increaseof Your Kingdom
among the scattered, the hurting, and the lost.
And Lord, please give grace to my brethren
to forgive me my messes
as I forgive them!
Amen.

Chapter 31

THE ALPHA AND THE OMEGA

Dearly Beloved,

"I am the Alpha and the Omega,
the first and the last,
the beginning and the end."
(Revelation 22:13)

The month of December, and the way we relate to all that it contains, makes us think of these words from Jesus. We look forward to the celebration of the birth of our Lord, which marks the beginning of God's complete and final revelation of Himself to us, and yet we also start looking back over the happenings of the nearly completed year. The beginning and the end . . . December is indeed the one month of the year in which we all tend to get rather sentimental, nostalgic, and somewhat introspective. The fact is, December is much more of a "take stock and inventory" month with most of us than January is.

Some of us are reminded that as children our behavior record for the past year determined if we would receive our reward around the Christmas tree. We anxiously wondered whether we had been judged "naughty or nice," or if nice, "nice enough?" Had we "measured up" to our parents' expectations, or (gulp) to God's? Did the scarcity (or the abundance) of gifts we would be receiving silently signify an accurate evaluation of our efforts, or the extent of our parents' love towards us, or of God's approval of us?

So with fear we formed the new "resolutions" in our

hearts and in our minds for the new year ahead. *"I'll start over again, and this year I'll do better, just you watch and see."* The meaning of Christmas was thus lost in focusing on our faults; the fear that we wouldn't receive what we wanted; and the concern that the presents we were planning to give were not sufficient to give the love-message we wanted to convey.

Jesus' words (John 10:10) were that He came to give us LIFE. So the enduring spirit of the Christian Christmas celebration should be focused on the coming of this New Life with each present we give and receive, with each greeting we minister, with each carol we sing, with each decoration we rehang, and with every special traditional function we attend or observe.

His birth as a human baby, His life as a spiritual man, and His death as the sacrificial lamb were orchestrated by the Holy Spirit at God's command to declare the end of an era of Satan's dominion and the beginning of the era of the Kingdom of God. It also marked the end of the old covenant and the beginning of the new—the new covenant which allows us former Gentiles to be included in God's promises to the righteous Jews. Now we are both invited into God's Kingdom through belief in Jesus Christ as the Son of God.

Hebrews 7:18–19 tells us: **"For, on the one hand, there is a setting aside of a former commandment because of its weakness and uselessness (for the Law made nothing perfect), and on the other hand there is a bringing in of a better hope, through which we draw near to God."**

His birth, life, death, and resurrection revealed the fact that God **"...appointed** [His Son] **heir of all things, through whom also He made the world. And** [Jesus] **is the radiance of** (God's) **glory and the exact**

representation of His nature . . ." (Hebrews 1:2–3). "**He is also head of the body, the church; and He is the beginning, the first-born from the dead; so that He Himself might come to have first place in everything.**" (Colossians 1:18)

This is Who is portrayed lying helplessly as a baby in the manger! He, "**who, although He existed in the form of God, did not regard equality with God a thing to be grasped, but emptied Himself, taking the form of a bond-servant, and being made in the likeness of men.**" (Philippians 2:6–7)

Some years ago, we wanted to express this exciting truth in a way that would be forever engraved on the minds and hearts of our children and the congregation of the church we were pastoring. The Lord heard our prayer and gave us graphic instructions. He directed us to build a simple wooden manger (two feet square, eight inches deep, and eighteen inches high) and fill it with nonflammable straw. Our children loved being part of such an exciting construction project, and zealously measured, sawed, glued, hammered, stained and sealed that precious little vessel. It looked beautiful!

On Christmas Eve we brought our lovingly-constructed little manger to our Christmas service and placed a tray with the Communion bread and wine on top of the straw. After blessing the bread and the wine, we invited the church to come forward in turn by families and friends, to kneel at the side of the manger, and to let their minds and spirits dwell on the birth of this little child whose destiny was to be their saving grace. We encouraged them to see this divine baby as the beginning of hope and the end of Satan's control over us—to see Him as the little lamb who was at the same time the awesome Lion of Judah—to see the cross beckoning to Him beyond the manger.

As we shared Communion with each other, we sensed the awesome flow of God's unfathomable love towards us—the love that was willing to die to pay the judgment against us, to ransom us from our sentence of death.

What a blessing to know that **"Jesus** [Himself] **has become the guarantee of a better covenant"** (Hebrews 7:22) by **"the power of an indestructible life."** (Hebrews 7:16) **"Hence, also, He is able to save forever those** [of us] **who draw near to God through Him, since He always lives to make intercession for** [us]**."** (Hebrews 7:25)

We took that precious manger home with us that Christmas Eve, and we hid our little love gifts to the children in the straw for them to find next morning. We had a very special experience that Christmas of our Father God's special love gift to us—His Son, Jesus! We have continued this as a family tradition ever since, and now our grandchildren are learning the scope of God's love at the side of this little manger—that Jesus is both the beginning and the end of faith and revelation of the Father.

Our prayer is that your Christmas memories will be wrapped up in the warm, sure, knowledge that **"the old things have passed away . . . new things have come."** (2 Corinthians 5:17) May **". . . mercy and peace and love be multiplied to you."** In Jesus' name! (Jude 2)

Hugs,

Paul & Gretel

Dear Heavenly Father,
help me to focus on the whole person of Jesus
this season of corporately celebrating
Your giving Him to us here on the earth!
Help me to see the Man in the Baby,
the Lion in the Lamb, the sacrifice in the gift!
Help me to filter out all of the worldly
clutter that has polluted the
simplicity and purity
of Jesus' birth.
Amen.

BIBLIOGRAPHY

Bruchko: by Bruce E. Olson, Creation House, Altamonte Springs, Florida, 1978; also Marshall, Morgan & Scott, London, England.

"Christianity Today": Christianity Today Inc., Carol Stream, Illinois.

Idioms in the Bible Explained and a Key to the Original Gospel: by George M. Lamsa, Harper & Row, Publishers, San Francisco, California, 1985.

Let Us Worship: by Judson Cornwall, Bridge Publishing, Inc., So. Plainfield, New Jersey, 1983.

"Renewal": Broadway House, Crowborough, East Sussex, England.

Root Out of a Dry Ground: A History of the Church: by Charles P. Schmitt, Fellowship Publications, Grand Rapids, Minnesota, 1979.

The Pleasure of His Company: by Roger C. Palms, Tyndale House Publishers, Inc., Wheaton, Illinois, 1982.

The American Heritage Dictionary: Houghton Mifflin Company, Boston, Massachusetts, 1978.

Webster's New Collegiate Dictionary: G. & C. Merriam Company, Springfield, Massachusetts, U.S.A., 1977.

Webster's New World Dictionary: Simon and Schuster, New York, New York, 1980.

If you have enjoyed this book and would like to help us to send a copy of it and many other titles to needy pastors in the **Third World**, please write for further information or send your gift to:

Sovereign World Trust
PO Box 777, Tonbridge
Kent TN11 9XT
United Kingdom

or to the **'Sovereign World'** distributor in your country.

If sending money from outside the United Kingdom, please send an International Money Order or Foreign Bank Draft in STERLING, drawn on a **UK** bank to **Sovereign World Trust**.

RESURRECTION CHRISTIAN MINISTRIES would be delighted to send you the monthly **LETTERS of FAITH** as they are published. Although we offer them free, we are most grateful to those who are sensitive enough to realize that some of our subscribers have to financially undergird our costs if we are to continue providing them free to others and to Third World saints and ministries.
We also invite inquiries as to our availability for ministering in churches, seminars, and retreats.
Address all such requests to the authors at:

Resurrection Christian Ministries
300 Eagles Nest Farm Rd.
Hawk Point, Missouri 63349 U.S.A.